D1524643

The ELL Critical Data Process

3rd Edition

Distinguishing between disability and language acquisition – a matrix based approach.

Knowing the critical data to gather, the staff to involve, and having a process to follow can increase the likelihood of appropriate intervention. This resource kit contains resources and guiding documents to help understand whether targeted interventions or a special education referral is the appropriate action for your student.

Steve Gill and Ushani Nanayakkara, Authors

©Steve Gill, Ushani Nanayakkara

Table of Contents

Acknowledgements

Steve and Ushani would like to thank the thousands of people who have worked with us over the years to help build the ELL Critical Data Process into a stronger process and make the process easier to complete with fidelity.

Preface

This book guides individuals along the path of the ELL Critical Data Process, both the K-12 Version and Preschool Version. The third edition was created to add some critical clarifications that increase the likelihood of accurate implementation, to greatly reduce the price by removing color content, and to add a new chapter on core instruction as related to interventions. In 2023, the third edition was revised to make updates to items 3, 9, and the matrix.

The information contained in this third edition revised of the ELL Critical Data Process reflects what we learned since first publishing on the ELL Critical Data Process. The questions from the over 21,000 educators, who were trained on the process to date, truly helped in improving the process and how the process is explained. The field of understanding which ELL students need to be evaluated for the possibility of special education qualification is sadly behind the times. There is very little solid research in this area, and the research is very limited in scope (e.g. Washington State alone, at last count, served over 200 languages in its ELL population, yet virtually all research into ELL/special education evaluation focuses on just one language, Spanish). It is important to note that at last count Spanish did account for roughly 75% of all ELL students in the United States.

The process you are about to learn is focused on helping staff to take a journey that allows them to learn more about the student, and to understand the student's needs at a much greater depth. The aim of the process is to help staff understand what the most appropriate intervention should be for the student. That intervention could be special education. However, we know that some groups are overrepresented, and a few sub portions of groups are potentially underrepresented in special education qualifications. Therefore, knowing the trends in your district is critical. If you have over representation of a group, it is reasonably likely that you have a systemic flaw. It is impossible to find well-constructed research that shows that any group has a statistically higher likelihood of a real disability in any category when the variables for each group are controlled.

The ELL Critical Data Process is widely used across the State of Washington and in several other states. The author has now trained over 21,000 educators on the process across too many districts to remember. The ELL Critical Data Process is being used in 12 countries that we know of at the time of writing this. The anecdotal reports have been positive to the extreme from all of the districts who have adopted this approach. Two recent comments that we have appreciated greatly are, "Learning this has changed my life as an educator!" and "Your training saved our district!" One of the districts I worked with was at 43% qualification rate for their language learners and is now (five years later) qualifying proportionally and providing needed interventions to address the needs of the students outside special education. Leading experts in the field reviewed the first edition of this book and told the authors that the work is "groundbreaking" work in the field. As noted above, many years later the process has spread across the United States and to other countries. Several districts have been able to share their improvements with data, and the district the author worked in had the "cleanest" data the author has seen to date. By "cleanest," we are referring to data that has very few areas of disproportionality and the areas that do exist have causes/reasons that we were aware of and worked on. Therefore, this work has led to taking a problem that was of unknown complexity and reducing it to four targeted areas of needed focus and improvement (e.g., over qualification of Spanish speaking students in the category of Specific Learning Disability). Teams are excited about having a process that helps them to understand the students and that greatly increases the likelihood of the student getting an intervention that is meaningfully related to the presenting problem. And, districts are learning to change programs to address the needs of their language learners.

Structure of the Book

Introduction --- Some history and brief coverage of what is to come.

LE³AP --- The matrix process in this book uses the lens of Looking at Exposure, Experience, Expectations and Practice. LE³AP helps people to look at a problem/concern and talk about whether or not there is something clearly missing in one of these areas (indicating a need for action to intervene in that area) or that there are no clear reasons for the problem/concern (indicating the possibility of a disability). Referrals are not because we know there is a disability, but instead because we suspect there is a disability as defined in special education regulations.

ELL Critical Data Process K-12 Version --- This is the process of gathering the critical data for kindergarten through 12th grade students and using a structured process to analyze the data. The group discussions, using the guide, lead to rating each piece of data from "supports more intervention" to "neutral" to "supports a referral". Then, the team will have a matrix, a visual representation, of the results of their discussion. These discussions lead the team to knowing whether or not a special education referral or more intervention(s) is/are the appropriate step. The discussions can also help the team to understand what interventions are needed, if more intervention(s) is/are called for, or guide the team toward the data needed to process a special education referral, if a special education referral is the result.

The SLD Mini-Matrix --- This is a mini-matrix that is critical when examining potential eligibility for students with less than 5 years of schooling in our system and is included within the 3rd edition of this book.

ELL Critical Data Process; Preschool Version --- The difference between this and the K-12 version is a stronger focus on Exposure, Experience, Expectations, and Practice (the LE³AP process). This is due to the fact that there is far less data available regarding a 3-5-year-old at this stage of the process.

School Building and District Data --- The questions that need to be answered and much of the data that needs to be collected to know where your disproportionality occurs, so that you know what challenges the team faces.

Belief Systems --- The authors and other professionals that provide training have noted that belief systems issues are some of the main reasons that disproportionality has not improved on a national level. Note that the data has not improved in a notable fashion since measuring disproportionality began decades ago. This section focuses on examples and research that help the reader understand the link between acculturation, belief systems, practices, and results. Our poor results are not due to practices that are purposefully targeted at creating disproportionality, therefore the poor results are due to subtle issues within our belief systems. These subtle beliefs are created from our acculturation and lack of knowledge in certain areas.

Special Education Categories: Problem Areas --- This is a short chapter to emphasize that disproportionality is primarily found within 3 disability categories.

Core Instruction, evidence/proof, then intervention --- This short chapter discusses the need to have core instruction targeting the specific core areas of language acquisition, then evidence/proof of the effectiveness, before the discussion of interventions can begin.

Appendices --- The appendices provide information related to some of the key quotes used in the book, a section on how data from this process can be directly related to specific interventions or supporting/not supporting evaluation data, comments on Steve's and Ushani's books, Steve's biography, comments on his training, and an overview of trainings offered by Steve.

How to use this Book

The authors recommend that you first read through the ELL Critical Data Process a couple of times and think about the process as presented in this book. We believe that doing this will lead to a higher level of understanding in the end, even though you will have a lot of questions at first.

This material is all about getting the right people to the table with the right data, and providing a guided process that will lead a team to understanding what the student really needs.

There are statements in these documents that are not universally agreed upon. For example, I believe that 50% of all students currently qualified for special education do not actually have disabilities, but are instead curriculum, methodology, system and/or instructional casualties. There are experts who have argued with me that the percentage is as high as 75%, and few people have posed arguments with no data/research that indicate a lower percentage. Please note, my argument is based upon the data from successful RTI implementation sites and the data from research on intensive interventions, in addition my work and experience in the field.

Remember to focus on the most important thing: using the process and the expertise of your staff to fully understand the root causes of the student's presenting problems, so that you are sure that the interventions are meaningful for the student.

Last, most people reading this come from either a special education background or an ELL background. It will be important to take note of the areas in which you need to do some follow-up research and do it. For most people with a special education background, language acquisition is an area that needs study. For most people with an ELL background, special education law and qualification are areas that need study.

Special Note: The authors at times are using native language, at times primary language, and at times both. When we work with parents and children, we need to know their language history such that we know what languages they have learned, the circumstances around learning those languages, and their literacy in each of the languages. For many of our families, this will not be an issue, given that their native language and primary language are one and the same. For other parents and children, this could make a difference and help us to understand the challenges they face, have faced and could face in the future. There are concepts noted in this book, like primary language versus native language, that drive the reason to have a variety of experts on your team. In order to know the "correct" answer for your setting, you need to have discussion. Prior to these discussions, make sure to find your state's definition of these in both the ELL context and the special education context. The definitions vary by state and within some states the two groups have different definitions.

You have permission to make copies and use the documents in this book as needed within your current setting (school site). The expectation is that each team has at least 1 copy of the book in order to use these materials and concepts.

The image quality in this book is lower than the image quality in the 2nd edition, given that we removed all of the color content. Therefore, the images that were originally in color lost some clarity. This was done to greatly reduce the cost of the book for the reader.

Chapter 1: Challenges and Problems

This chapter addresses some of the challenges faced in this work and some of the problems faced when attempting to solve those problems. Each topic in this chapter relates to the overall work but does not always relate to the prior topic or the following topic.

Some of the Problems in This Field

After a short introduction, this book starts with the Matrix Process for assessing students, then provides other critical information educators need to be successful in working with their teams and their own belief systems. If you want to jump straight into the meat of the process, go ahead and skip to reading about the ELL Critical Data Process for right now, but do come back to read the introduction. The job of processing referrals is a difficult and stressful job, even with good people wanting to do a good job. The data from schools with strong RTI/MTSS programs shows us that we test and qualify far too many children (RTI is Response to Intervention and MTSS is Multi-Tiered Systems of Support). Comments like this will have more clarity after reading the remainder of the book.

Education is possibly the field of work that takes the longest to react to research and implement changes. A large part of this, in the authors' opinion, is due to subtle belief systems. If you would like to read research that supports this opinion, Dan C. Lortie was one of the first researchers in this area and others have agreed with his key findings.

Since beginning in the field of school psychology, Steve has read each and every book he could find, and articles/papers, about what one should and should not do when evaluating language learners. Yet, after 30 years of working in this area, there is still very little work addressing the challenges. The SLD Mini-Matrix is extremely rare in this field, given it is focused on helping the working school psychologist during real/actual day-to-day work. This problem is most prevalent with students who might qualify under the category of Specific Learning Disability. A goal of this book is to reduce the likelihood that a practitioner feels unsure at the end of the evaluation. Please note, some practitioners currently believe that what they are doing is solid practice, even though their practices lead to extremely disproportionate rates of qualification. After working with more than 1,500 school districts and training over 21,000 educators, staff members, and practitioners on the ELL Critical Data Process and related ELL/Special Education issues, Steve can honestly state that not a single district he has worked with actually knew their disproportionality issues beyond the most superficial of levels. Few educators know that the Specific Learning Disability category tripled from 1975 to 2000/2004 and accounted for 50% of all students qualified for special education services. Since then, the category of Specific Learning Disability has decreased from 50% to 38.8% and continues to drop, all while RTI/MTSS has become more prevalent. Within this book there are notes that the exact percentage of students qualified in this category is difficult to know (more information to come).

Don't Use the "R" Word Unless You Really Mean It...

Within the schools, staff members may talk about referring a student for a special education evaluation, without really knowing what that entails. It is important to discuss the legal meaning of a referral with all staff. Do not imply that a referral needs to wait when a staff member truly wants to make a referral. Instead, help them understand that in many cases a special education evaluation is very difficult to process with accuracy when there is no history of targeted interventions, when there is no evidence of a targeted intervention that has shown to be successful for like peers, or there is no evidence of "core" instruction in the area of concern. This is far more critical for students who are suspected of having a specific learning disability than it is for children with blindness. The area of specific learning disability is the most overused area with our ELL students and is the category that is the most difficult to do correctly with our ELL qualified students. In contrast, we rarely qualify students for special education, who have blindness, who don't really need the services that special education can provide. As you will see, the work by Dr. Carnine, Dr. Torgesen, and the impact of RTI/MTSS on qualification rates helps us to understand that our accuracy is not as high with students with learning disabilities.

Disproportionality

Disproportionality is common within special education and gifted/highly capable programs. In a nutshell, the students within either of these groups do not match the demographics of your school or your district. For example, if 12% of your students are Black/African American and 19% of your students are Hispanic/Latino, then within both special education and gifted/highly capable programs approximately 12% of the students should be Black/African American and approximately 19% should be Hispanic/Latino. This is not what is occurring in the vast majority of school districts, nor in any state that the authors have heard of, nor in the data for the United States as a whole. In addition to the disproportionality within special education, there is significant disproportionality within gifted education. Sadly, it is virtually the mirror opposite of the disproportionality found in special education, and is a real-life example of institutional racism. Furthermore, since the data on disproportionality has been measured, there have not been positive changes at the national level. We can either be part of maintaining this problem, making this problem worse, or be part of the solution. This book, in addition to our other books, are meant to help you understand these problems while providing you practical actions to take in order to be part of the solution.

The following quote from the NASP Communique, Vol 38, #1, September 2009 provides evidence of the depth of these problems.

> *Black students, particularly those identified as mentally retarded or emotionally disabled, have been consistently overrepresented for more than 3 decades. Native American students are also persistently overrepresented in special education nationally, and while the same is*

not true for Latino students, they are often overrepresented at the state and district levels where their enrollment is highest.

Special education identification patterns vary both between and within states. For instance, risk for Black students identified as mentally retarded is more than 14 times that of their White peers in some states while risk is nearly equivalent in others.

The disproportionality literature tends to focus on the disability categories of mental retardation, learning disabilities, and emotional disabilities, as these are the high-incidence disabilities and constitute over 63% of students eligible for special education (U.S. Department of Education [USDOE], 2009). These are also widely regarded as "judgmental" categories because of relatively vague federal and state disability definitions that necessitate a high degree of professional judgment in making normative comparisons to determine eligibility (Klingner et al., 2005). This has led many to question the validity of these diagnoses as true disabilities and the likelihood of misidentification, particularly in light of the wide variation in identification rates across states and districts. In contrast, diagnoses in the low-incidence categories are rarely challenged because of their physical/medical bases, and because disproportionality is not generally observed in these categories.

Applicable Laws and the Issues that Arise from Those Laws

Our laws provide guidelines and/or requirements that we are expected to follow, yet our data clearly shows that we are not following some of these laws, or that we are not looking at our data to see if our results show whether or not we are following the laws.

The laws expect that a student is not to be qualified for special education if the presenting problem can be addressed in general education with or without accommodations and modifications. Yet our results show that we have far more students receiving special education services than can be supported by data and research. Also, as RTI and MTSS have grown, specific learning disability qualification has greatly decreased. This indicates that, if we meet the needs of the students within the general education system, many would not have been incorrectly identified as having a disability.

Throughout this book the Washington Administrative Codes (WAC) are used given that the authors are based in Washington State. The CFRs (federal special education laws) have the same content for each law that is noted, and all state special education laws are based upon the CFRs.

> ▸ WAC 392-172A-01035

> ▸ "Intellectual disability, a hearing impairment (including deafness), a speech or language impairment, a visual impairment (including blindness), an emotional behavioral disability, an orthopedic impairment, autism, traumatic brain injury, other health impairment, a specific learning disability, deaf-blindness, multiple disabilities, or for students, three through eight, a developmental delay and who, because of the disability and adverse educational impact, **has unique needs that cannot be addressed exclusively through education in general education classes with or without individual accommodations,** and needs special education and related services."

(This wording was added in Washington state law. Bold was added for emphasis.)

The Washington State law clearly states that a child is not to be found eligible for something that can be addressed within the general education setting. Therefore, if the school is implementing targeted interventions and those interventions are working, then the student (in almost all cases) should not be considered for or qualified for special education. The CFRs are not as bold on this statement, yet there are many indications in the CFRs that the same expectation is to be met.

Furthermore, the laws regarding appropriate instruction and language acquisition add another set of factors that must be addressed. We are supposed to be able to rule out a lack of appropriate instruction in reading and/or math and limited English proficiency as determining factors in creating the struggles the student is demonstrating. This can be near impossible at times, yet we can gather data across a variety of sources that creates a case, when carefully considered and documented, that a stranger to the situation will understand as reasonable.

- WAC 392-172A-03040
- "(2)(a) A student **must not be determined to be eligible** for special education services **if** the determinant factor is:

> (i) **Lack of appropriate instruction in reading**, based upon the state's grade level standards;
>
> (ii) **Lack of appropriate instruction in math**; or
>
> (iii) **Limited English proficiency**; and

> (b) If the student does not otherwise meet the eligibility criteria including presence of a disability, adverse educational impact and need for specially designed instruction.
> (3) In interpreting evaluation data for the purpose of determining eligibility for special education services, each school district must:
> (a) Draw upon information from a variety of sources, including aptitude and achievement tests, parent input, and teacher recommendations, as well as information about the student's physical condition, social or cultural background, and adaptive behavior; and
> (b) Ensure that information obtained from all of these sources is documented and carefully considered."

Issues around appropriate instruction, Limited English Proficiency, a variety of sources, and social or cultural background are all issues that often receive little or no attention within the evaluation reports for those students who have the most prevalent challenges in these areas. At times, there is a great deal of pressure to "make" students eligible when staff cannot or will not recognize other issues and look for other solutions. Lack of appropriate instruction in reading and/or math is not just an ELL issue. How can you teach "appropriate" reading and math to students who do not know the language or are just developing the language? The techniques found within GLAD* and SIOP*, and other techniques, can reduce the impact of not knowing the language. However, even with those, can we reach the bar of "appropriate"? What is our data showing us? Are the students in your school getting appropriate instruction in reading and/or math if less than 50% are passing the state tests? Or 40%? Or 30%? Or 20%?

*GLAD and SIOP are both systems/techniques used in the classroom to increase the likelihood that the lesson is comprehensible by the student. For example, having a picture of an apple when you are talking about an apple and/or using that same apple during a lesson on fractions by cutting it into pieces to represent fractions.

One last important note regarding these laws is the following. Confusion occurs with staff around the concept of "adverse impact" and the words adverse impact. The concept "adverse impact" is about how a disability is creating an adverse impact on the child's ability to access their education and that requires special education services. The confusion is that these children are doing poorly in school. Therefore, staff have often related the words adverse impact to the concept "adverse impact" by thinking that adverse impact is synonymous with doing poorly in school. However, doing poorly in school could be related to the many other issues discussed in this book, and could have no relationship to a disability. Therefore, the legal use of "adverse impact" requires the ability to directly relate the struggles the student is having to the documented disability in order to qualify the student for special education services.

The WAC has added "adverse impact" to all of the disability categories. The CFR has this for most, but not all, categories. However, the wording throughout the CFR supports the concept of adverse impact determination for all disability categories.

A Belief of the Authors

There is no doubt that disproportionality in special education has existed for at least 40 years and has changed little over those 40 years. Educators are good and caring people, because becoming an educator certainly is not about the money. Knowing this, one must wonder why we have such discrepant numbers and results. It is the belief of the authors that we have been trained, acculturated, in very subtle ways throughout our lives to have beliefs that we are not aware of or do not know the impact of. And, with "our" we mean all of us. The problems are subtle, and the most subtle of impacts of prejudice play themselves out in ways we are unaware of in our lives. The examples within this book can help us see our results, then maybe we will also see our practices, belief systems, and acculturation as interrelated.

The following quote was taken from a report to congress:

"Using data from the U.S. Department of Education, analyses suggest that Black children are 2.88 times more likely than White children to be labeled as having mental retardation and 1.92 times more likely to be labeled as having an emotional/behavioral disorder (Losen & Orfield, 2002). Research suggests that unconscious racial bias, stereotypes, inequitable implementation of discipline policies, and practices that are not culturally responsive may contribute to the observed patterns of identification and placement for many minority students."

> Information from the *Twenty-fourth Annual Report to Congress on the Implementation of the Individuals with Disabilities Education Act (IDEA)* (U.S. Department of Education, 2002), available at: http://www2.ed.gov/about/reports/annual/osep/2002/index.html

The later chapter on belief systems will address this at greater length and provide people with ways to examine these issues. Steve, who provides training and consultation with school districts, has experienced these issues across numerous districts. Also, Steve heard Clay Cook, a leader in MTSS work, talk about first working with districts on belief systems before working on structural issues. So, go ahead and start with the dessert (the process), but please do not forget to read and process the information on belief systems.

The following example is based on special education qualification rates in Washington State. It will help you see how much impact individuals and subtle biases can have, considering that almost all of the noted districts are extremely small school districts. The data from the following research provides a concrete example of biases impacting our practices and our results. These results demonstrate profound differences that are extremely unlikely to have happened by chance, and extremely unlikely to have happened by purposeful, harmful actions.

Special Education Qualification Rates in Washington State

Steve examined the data for 295 school districts. No district was purposely left out of the data, with the exception of school districts in the data set that were(are) not actually comprehensive school districts (e.g., School for the Blind). Therefore, with a set of 250 districts, it is highly unlikely that any district missed would have impacted the noted trends.

For 16 districts the special education eligibility percentages fell below 10% of the total student population. For 15 of these 16 school districts, the average student population in the districts was 145 students (145 is the average of the total student population and not just the total for the special education population; the 16th was a medium sized district noted separately below).

There were 32 districts with special education eligibility percentages above 18% of the total student population. The average student population across these districts was 392 students. As above, 392 represents the total student population and not just the special education population. The highest percentage of children qualified as children with disabilities was 37.5% of the district. Can there really be a district where 37.5% of the children have disabilities? That district happened to have a population in which 75% of the students were of Native American heritage. Did those two numbers happen together totally by chance? That is very unlikely, and the results are inappropriate.

In the State of Washington, 45.9% of the students were on Free or Reduced Lunch at the time of this research. The average percentage of F/R Lunch for the districts below 10% special education qualification rate was 24%. The average percentage of F/R Lunch for the districts above 18% was 75.6%.

The only medium/large district with a percentage below 10% of the student population qualified for special education services was the Issaquah School District, at 8.8%. It is interesting to note that Issaquah School District has some of the highest state test scores noted during this research.

Although the F/R Lunch difference is extreme, there is no way to prove that it is a causal factor. Yet, many research studies have indicated that poverty is a very high predictor of special education qualification. This occurs even though it would be very hard to argue, beyond a minimal percentage difference, that poverty has any correlation to rates of disabilities, and no causal relationship either. It is important to note that the causal or correlational issues we are talking about are the parents of our children, not our children. Therefore, the correlation becomes far weaker when looking at the children. That is, the small correlation of the parent in poverty to disability of the parent would be multiplied by the small correlation of parent to child disability (inheritance) to achieve a very small correlational value/predictive value.

It is interesting to note that virtually all of the districts on the extremes of the range have very small student populations. In all of these cases, one or only a few people are leading the qualification decisions.

It would be hard to examine this data and not see the human impact on the work. We have a lot of power in influencing outcomes, and, hopefully, a lot to think about in our daily work to bring about positive student outcomes.

You will see these points repeated throughout the book because we have a very hard time seeing ourselves involved in any of the negative results ("we" being that universal we). However, most staff have not examined the data for their schools and district. We need to have the courage to look closely at our work and to begin to solve problems as they appear. The data is not the way it is because, so few people are involved in the problem. Wherever there is a problem, a lot of staff members were involved in creating or maintaining the problem (remember, not bad people, just bad results). This could seem to contradict what was said above. However, in the problem noted above just a few people had "control" over the outcome, yet many people had input and involvement. So, the big "we" could have stopped the problem if they had seen it as a problem. We need as many people as possible involved in the solutions.

Part of being the solution is asking your state for the data (many examples of the types of data are noted in this book), and then knowing your building and district data. Make the comparisons and share the knowledge with your teams.

More evidence of "our" impact:

▶ "SLD numbers may have dropped due to the proliferation of Response to Intervention (RTI)—a method of providing targeted assistance to young children who have difficulty learning—and other early-reading interventions (see *Response to Intervention*). Lastly, the identification of SLDs, though strictly outlined in policy, appears more subjective and **prone to human error** than the identification of most other disabilities; thus, SLD identification is perhaps more affected by related changes in policy, budget, personnel, etc."

▶ Source --- Fordham Institute Article on Trends

The words in bold from the quote above (bold added for emphasis), need to be challenged. School psychologists have long been described as the "gate keepers" of special education, yet Steve has found very few that like or appreciate this role. The words in bold, in Steve's experience, are not quite correct. It is often not human error (an error in judgment or a mistake). For example, Steve has seen school psychologists give students two different IQ tests and two different academic tests, and then mix and match across the tests until they find a discrepancy (discrepancy model for SLD). This is not done by error. These school psychologists know that this approach is inappropriate; however, they feel a great deal of pressure by the administration and teachers to qualify students. Therefore, it is a bad choice and not a mistake/human error.

As noted above, many of us have been involved in the system that created and maintained the poor results that are so common across our nation. Now, we need to have everyone involved in the solutions.

A key question

Again, we all need to ask ourselves whether we are part of creating these problems, sustaining these problems, or solving these problems. As you read this book, please keep this in mind. Also, please understand that it is virtually impossible to be part of the solution, if you don't know your own data, the data of your school, and the data of your district. That is, how can you know if you are part of solving the problem if you don't know what or where the problem is….

Chapter 2: LE³AP

Look at:

Exposure

Experience

Expectations

and

Practice

Introduction

The LE³AP lens is explained to a greater extent in the following stories taken from our book, ***Processing Perspectives: Examining Beliefs, Biases, and Reality Through Stories.*** These stories help emphasize for the reader the powerful impact our practices can have on our students. The description of the LE³AP process is then followed by real life examples of applying this lens to students during the pre-referral, referral and/or evaluation process.

Stories

Some groups of our language learners are qualified for special education at much higher rates, and this indicates that many students without disabilities are seen as children with disabilities. This often leads to them not getting the actual services they need. These stories are about children who were negatively impacted by our system. We are good and caring people, as educators, so these results are unacceptable.

Things to think about when reading these stories:

- As you read this, can you relate to it personally?
- Have you ever worked with a student, colleague or parent who was similar?
- What messages did you send to that student, colleague, or parent verbally or non-verbally?
- How do you believe they remember you?
- How would you like to be remembered by them?
- What did you do to make their life better?
- What did you do that might not have made their life better?

Our Language Learners and Special Education

I happen to be a bilingual school psychologist in a medium to large sized school district. Over the years, I have seen many, many Spanish speaking students qualified for special education or recommended for special education evaluation in complete error. And, these students are not getting the language support that they need to be successful. Here are a few examples.

"I already know how to read in Spanish"

The first student who I am going to talk about was in high school when I was asked to complete a bilingual evaluation. I was invited by the building school psychologist after this student told her, "I don't know why you people have me in this class, I already know how to read and write in Spanish."

This student came to the United States in the seventh grade and was placed into special education. There was more to the story and the original team didn't get everything wrong; however, nobody looked at what this student could do, only at what he "couldn't do in English." It didn't take long until they moved this student into a self-contained special education classroom. In this classroom, he was working on letter sounds and letter names. The school psychologist was impressed by this young man and his conviction, enough so that she believed he might be telling her the truth regarding his skills. However, she had no way to measure them.

I completed the evaluation. This student was reading at the 10th grade level in Spanish, and his math was at the highest level in which he had instruction (the 6th grade level). Therefore, he was spending day after day in an environment that was totally inappropriate for him. I wonder what his teachers were thinking along the way? How was it that nobody noticed this until now? If it were not for his efforts to self-advocate, nobody would have ever known about his skills, just his deficits in a language he had only recently started to learn.

He wants to be a teacher someday.

Learning disability in one language and not the other?

This little boy was in the second grade in a bilingual education school. The school psychologist invited me in to complete core academic testing with this student. The teachers were convinced that he had a learning disability. The testing showed his core academic skills, when testing was completed in Spanish, were at the third-grade level. Still, the teachers struggled to believe that he didn't have a learning disability. It would be pretty darn hard to have a learning disability in one language and not the other.

No formal education

In this example, the student was already qualified for special education and the school psychologist wanted to see how he would perform if tested in his native language. This student stated that he did not know how to read in Spanish, and he had no formal education in Spanish. The school psychologist had tested numerous students who have said the same thing, and the norm is that they try to read the Spanish as though it is English. However, this student demonstrated early reading skills in Spanish. If it were not for learned helplessness that he demonstrated at school and in the testing, it is likely that he would have performed at the mid-second grade level in reading in Spanish.

I began the intelligence testing in Spanish. He performed in the average range on the subtests that did not require verbal comprehension as part of the response. The testing showed that he did not have strong enough vocabulary in Spanish to be able to perform in Spanish on an IQ test (across all subtests). This is pretty common if a student has not received formal education in their native language and/or is not literate in their native language.

Stephen Krashen, a leading expert in language acquisition, states that our higher-level vocabulary and language structures develop through reading. So, I went on to test this student in receptive and expressive vocabulary using a test that is designed to be a Spanish-English Bilingual test. He scored well below the average for vocabulary, which again, was what was expected (i.e., he didn't have the exposure, nor the experience needed to develop these skills in both languages). He needed to work on core vocabulary in both languages in order to have a high likelihood of success.

I talked to the student about how I learned to speak Spanish using the recommendations of Stephen Krashen. It is all about comprehensible input, which can occur via reading books at your level and moving upward with success. The student came back the following day and told me that he had told his mother about this idea, and she sent him straight to the library to get books in Spanish. This student has a huge desire to learn, and his parents have a huge desire for him to learn and be successful. They just needed ideas regarding what will help him to make better progress.

He doesn't speak that language

This last example might be the most unusual, strange, sad case that I have seen. I was a lead for the school psychologists when I got a call from one of the school psychologists in a little bit of a panic. There was a student who had enrolled, and the paperwork indicated that he needed a self-contained special education setting for students with severe disabilities. The school psychologist met the student, and the boy didn't present like this at all. Students who need a restrictive placement such as this usually struggle with communication skills (in general, not language learning) and social skills, and this student didn't present this way.

The school psychologist went on to get an interpreter, to try to get to the bottom of this mystery. The previous school district had evaluated this student after 2 months in the country. They found him to have a severe intellectual disability and to be in need of this type of placement. Sadly, they had made two huge, impactful errors.

First, this student (an eighth grader when he arrived in our district 18 months later) had never been in school before. Second, as a child moving to California from Mexico, the school assumed that he spoke Spanish. So, all interactions with him had been in Spanish (leading to the special education evaluation). Also, the special education evaluation was all done in Spanish. However, he did not speak nor understand a single word of Spanish. Imagine how you would do if evaluated in a language in which you did not understand a single word.

We ended up having to "punt" in this situation. There was no program that was right for him, but we knew for sure that a self-contained special education program placement for a student who presented as cognitively normal was not the right decision. We created a truly one-off program for him in his school. Sadly, he moved sixth months later. We were able to right one wrong, but I don't know if we got him far enough along the right path with our work.

Evaluating language learners for special education services is a very difficult task to do correctly. Also, we have a lot of disproportionality within our language learners, and it is mostly over qualification of certain student groups within certain disability categories. It is clear that we need to do a better job, and each and every one of us needs to look at language learners first with a lens of what they can do. This will help us better understand the meaning of the skills they are not yet demonstrating.

Reflection:

Now that you have read these stories and thought about the questions, it is time to reflect.

- What did you think about when you read this?
- How can that help you in dealing with current and future students?
- How can that help you in dealing with current and future parents?
- How can that help you in dealing with current and future colleagues?
- What can you do differently starting today, to achieve better results (even if you started with good results)?

The LE³AP Process – Real Life Examples

The following is the application of the LE³AP process to real life situations.

The LE³AP process takes into account these four main areas, in order to understand whether the skill deficit in question is related to Exposure, Experience, Expectations, and Practice versus a possible disability. In other words, once a team has looked at a problem with the "lens" of exposure, experience, expectations and practice, does the presenting problem appear (all things considered) reasonable or does it appear to represent a potential disability?

These four areas are being differentiated as follows:

Exposure: The team looks at whether or not the student was exposed to the area of concern in a manner similar to students who have learned the skill/behavior in question.

Experience: Is differentiated by looking at whether or not the student was actively involved in the skill/behavior similar to students who developed the skill/behavior in question.

Expectation(s): Did the adults in the student's environment expect them to attempt/learn the new skill/behavior? How did they support that learning? And how do those expectations and support compare with what you would normally see for a child who has learned that skill/behavior?

Practice: Examines what the student (or adults) did in order for the student to get better at the skill/behavior and how that compares to students who have acquired the skill/behavior in question. Practice is a focused effort on improving a skill, not solely active participation in the skill/activity (e.g., working on phoneme skills development versus pleasure reading). Practice can be equated to intervention in many cases.

It is important to note that some students do not have exposure and/or experience given that they have a disability that limited their exposure and/or experience. For a student who clearly has a medical condition that impacts their access to their education or for a student who clearly has a cognitive impairment (referring to students who are likely to have intelligence test scores in the 50-60 or lower range), a process like this should be abbreviated as appropriate (based upon the documented evidence). In this case, the process might become more about data gathering for the referral and potential evaluation process (based upon facts, not impressions).

The following five examples provide some context.

Student 1:

This student was a 6th grade student who was performing well below grade level expectations. He is from a Russian background, and he is one of many siblings. The majority of his siblings were doing well in school, yet a few were doing poorly. All indicators were leading toward a special education referral. The school psychologist was in the process of interviewing the student's mother, and the information continued to support the possibility of a special education referral. Then, his mother stated, "You know he can read and write in Russian, right?" This information was not known to the team, so the school psychologist asked if they could use the interpreter to get an example of her son's reading and writing skills in Russian.

The student came into the school psychologist's office and the school psychologist opened a webpage in Russian, asking the student to read the information and provide a summary. The student did this and the interpreter stated that the summary was accurate. Then, the school psychologist wrote questions in English that the interpreter did not get to see. The student wrote responses to the questions in Russian and the interpreter read these. She stated that the written responses were easy to understand, just with some misspellings. The school psychologist asked the student's mother about the family's emphasis on English versus Russian. The student had 1 hour per week of class in Russian. The mother made it clear that it is very important to the family that the student learns to read and write in Russian, and that it is not so important that he reads and writes in English. They have a family business in which all of the boys are expected to work, and they need to be able to speak, read, and write in Russian for the business.

Exposure: The student has been exposed to English since very early in his life.

Experience: The student has been in an English school since Kindergarten and was participating at a low level.

Expectations: The family expects Russian skills to be learned and mastered, not English skills.

Practice: The student had a long history of completing very little work within the school setting.

Knowing all of this, is it really reasonable to expect him to have grade level skills in English???

And, a student who can read/write in their native language at a higher level than in English (with far less exposure and experience) is not a student with a learning disability.

Student 2:

A child 3 to 4 years of age is having a very difficult time pronouncing their words and does not appear to even be trying. When this child wants some cereal, their mom or dad or older sibling goes to the cupboard because the child is pointing that direction and grunting. Then, they open the cupboard and the adult (or older sibling) points to the first box. The child says, "untuh." The adult or older sibling points to the second box. The child says, "untuh." Then the third box, and the child responds, "unhuh."

The adult or older sibling then pulls this box down, fills a bowl with cereal and gives it to the child. The child has had their needs met without using appropriate language skills.

Exposure: It is highly likely that the child has heard all of the correct words.

Experience: The child has not been using or attempting to use the correct words.

Expectations: The adults are not expecting the child to use or attempt to use the correct words.

Practice: The child is not practicing the needed skills, neither approximations that could be shaped nor the actual words.

This child could be a child with a disability or non-disability developmental delay, yet it would be very difficult to accurately assess this skill set, not knowing what some intervention and work with the family could achieve.

Student 3:

A fourth-grade boy was having a very difficult time with reading comprehension. His entire family (other than his siblings) spoke zero English and his family stayed within the Latino community to get all of their needs met. His parents are literate in Spanish, but had told him that they didn't want him learning to read in Spanish until after he had learned to read in English without problems. The team talked with the parents and the parents agreed to allow the school psychologist, who happens to read in Spanish, to work with him on Spanish reading skills. In about 6 weeks, the boy was reading with comprehension, with most of the teaching regarding letter sounds. He then was able to comprehend at a higher level in Spanish than in English. It turned out that his basic language skills (i.e., BICS) were primarily in Spanish and his academic language skills (i.e., CALP) were primarily in English. It was very difficult for him to use contextual clues while reading in English, given he was missing many of the words. Yet, in Spanish he knew the words and could use them to figure out the more difficult words using contextual clues.

Exposure: He was exposed to the English words.

Experience: He did not use his English skills much, given he had no use for them outside of school. Within the school setting, there are many words that one is unlikely or less likely to use.

Expectations: Parents expected him to learn in English before developing the skill in Spanish.

Practice: There was no practice that was addressing the core problem, given that the core problem was not known.

This student benefitted greatly from the intervention that was focused on his actual need. This "practice" allowed him the opportunity to understand how to use contextual clues, using his stronger language. Then, he was able to transfer this skill into his work in English.

Student 4:

This student was also a fourth-grade student, and actually happened to be in the same classroom as student number 3. This student was having a very specific problem, he was struggling greatly with phonics and phonemes when reading. His parents were reading to him in Spanish and trying to work with him on these issues. His little sister (same environment as him) was in the second grade and already reading at a higher level than this student. Also, his parents were the only people in his world who spoke Spanish 100% of the time, his other relatives usually spoke English.

Exposure: He had been exposed to reading in English and had multiple years of intervention for the problems/concerns he was demonstrating.

Experience: He was trying to read in English and in Spanish, with support in both languages.

Expectations: His parents and school staff all had high expectations of him. His writing was at grade level, if spelling was not taken into account, his math calculations were at grade level independently, and his math problem solving was at grade level when the problems were read to him.

Practice: He had had several years of intervention that was designed to target his problems with phonics and phonemes.

This student was referred for a special education evaluation. His problem was very specific in nature and was showing up across both languages. He had been exposed to the skill that he was not developing, he had experience with these skills, he was expected to learn these skills, and he was given an intervention (practice) designed to improve these skills. These facts, along with the fact that his sister (same environment, two years younger) was reading at a higher-grade level than him, were all factors that helped determine that he was a student in need of special education services.

Student 5:

Soon after arriving in the United States, a parent came into the school and made a special education referral for her son prior to his first day of school. The school psychologist visited with her and talked about how unusual that was, explaining that we normally allow the student to start school, that we try to get to know the student, and then determine an appropriate action plan. She explained, through an interpreter she had brought with her, that her son had autism and was severely impacted. She had a stack of medical records and reports (all translated into English), and she wanted a special education evaluation. The school psychologist asked her to bring him to school later that day, to get an opportunity to meet him. She was very hesitant, believing that this was a very bad idea. She did bring him into the school later that day, and the school psychologist observed that he was, indeed, extremely impacted due to his autism.

Exposure: This child had had very little exposure to school and to his new environment.

Experience: This child had had no experience with a school in the new environment.

Expectations: He was expected to behave appropriately and to attempt to learn, but at this time the impact of his autism limited his success greatly.

Practice: There was very little practice that was occurring, given it was very difficult to obtain and maintain his attention on the wanted behaviors.

This student did not have the exposure, experience, nor practice. However, he was severely impacted by his disability and the fact that he did not speak English was not the determining factor in this situation. He was qualified for special education services within 10 school days.

Summary

These examples provide a glimpse into using the LE³AP process. This framework is meant to help staff look at problems based upon examining what is reasonable or likely, given exposure/experience/expectations/practice. Also, these steps provide information that helps staff reason through the design of potential interventions, or develop reasoning for the referral process, and/or develop reasoning and data for the evaluation process. Last, the final example demonstrates that, at times, the disability is the determinant factor and not the lack of English language development.

Applying this to Your Evaluation Process

The key to applying this to your evaluation process is using this information to write content that helps a stranger to the situation understand why you and your team made the decision, regarding the determinant factor. The following information is taken from our workbook that supplements our book on the ELL Critical Data Process and provides an example of applying this type of logic to defending the decision the team made. This information was part of the report for a language learner who was qualified for special education services under the category of specific learning disability. There are more examples in the following chapters.

Example:

The following section contains additional information that specifically addresses the fact that Esteban is an English Language Learner and that the difficulties he is demonstrating could be primarily related to this fact or could be primarily related to being a student with a disability. Additionally, the following information is meant to provide the reader context when trying to determine if language acquisition or disability is the determinant factor for Esteban's academic difficulties.

1) When Esteban is compared directly with two of his peers who speak the same language and entered kindergarten with similar ELPA-21 (language acquisition test) scores, Esteban has lost ground relative to his peers each year. That is, Esteban's test scores have actually decreased, and their test scores have increased. Esteban, when compared to his same age peers on this test, is not advancing. In contrast, one of his peers has made average growth and another has made exceptional growth within this environment. All three students speak Spanish, were born in the United States, and none of them have formal education in Spanish.

2) Esteban's younger sister is a student here at Somewhere Elementary. She is currently performing within the average range, and she is demonstrating skills similar to or stronger than Esteban's skills, even though she is two years younger.

3) Esteban is an English Language Learner and there is a high likelihood that this fact is impacting his growth in the areas of reading, math and written language. Esteban was not tested in Spanish in these areas, given that he has very limited abilities to perform in Spanish and prefers to use English whenever possible. At Somewhere Elementary, there are thirty students currently qualified as language learners and of these only two are qualified for special education services (those two were qualified prior to moving to Somewhere Elementary). Therefore, the team at Somewhere Elementary does not test to qualify language learners for special education services and the team at Somewhere Elementary stated that Esteban was their student of most concern amongst current ELL qualified students. The school has achieved these results even though the ELL program is not clearly defined. This indicates that Esteban's performance is different than his like peers and that he is having more difficulties than other language learners in this environment.

4) The ELL Critical Data Process was completed to better understand Esteban's history. There are no clear factors that were noted within this process that indicated that more intervention was clearly needed prior to determining disability. This process also did not uncover clear factors indicative of disability (e.g., a medical condition unknown to the team prior to starting). Esteban does have an older brother who struggled to progress and needed a great deal of additional help. The family has indicated that this brother is doing much better at this point in time.

5) On the MAP testing in reading and in math, Esteban has consistently scored at the 1st to 4th percentile in reading and in math. Of the two comparison students, both of whom entered Somewhere Elementary at the same time as Esteban and had similar ELPA-21 scores, one of the students has progressed from very low percentile scores to scores in the 35-45 percentile range, and the other has reached into the 55-65 percentile range. Each of these students has received similar intervention in reading over time, and the other two students in this direct comparison, have responded positively to the interventions.

6) Esteban has demonstrated some language confusion when spoken to in Spanish. However, Esteban has shown a strong preference towards English. Esteban's parents state that he rarely speaks in Spanish. During the evaluation process Esteban was willing to attempt to interact with the school psychologist in

Spanish, but stated that he prefers to speak English. Therefore, the presence of language confusion does not help in determining disability, given his exposure and experience with Spanish.

7) Esteban's teachers and parents have been able to establish and reinforce high expectations for Esteban, and the interviews indicate Esteban works hard to meet these expectations (see teacher comments as an example). Esteban's parents also commented that he is a very hard worker and that he is eager to learn in school. Esteban has been engaged in the learning process each and every time the school psychologist has entered the room.

8) Esteban's PE teacher and Music teachers both gathered data over a 10-week period of time regarding how well Esteban appeared to be learning the lessons in their classrooms compared to four of Esteban's peers. Esteban's scores during this are within the average of the other students. Esteban's PE teacher and Music teacher both commented on his efforts in class in a very positive manner.

9) Esteban's father is literate in Spanish and he did read to him in Spanish as a younger child. Therefore, Esteban had exposure to vocabulary in Spanish from his parents that is more extensive (i.e., individuals with literacy use a wider variety of vocabulary and more complex vocabulary). Esteban, as noted earlier in the report, uses English as his primary language. Therefore, Esteban has the exposure to this vocabulary, yet not the experience with the vocabulary, given he struggles to express himself in Spanish (e.g., Esteban can understand requests and simple conversation in Spanish, yet struggles when the vocabulary is more advanced relative to a student his age, and only expresses himself using very simple sentences and vocabulary in the present tense or present progressive tense). Esteban expressed himself without difficulties in English.

10) Esteban, during observation, remained engaged in the learning environment.

In Summary: Is the determinant factor a disability or language acquisition with a disability? Your job is to create a document, your report, that can be read by a stranger and the result is the stranger to the situation knows what data/evidence you used, what your decision was, and they believe that the conclusion you came to is supported by the data/evidence you have documented. Remember, if you didn't include the information, data, evidence within your reasoning (in your report), then it doesn't exist from a legal point of view.

Chapter 3: ELL Critical Data Process - K-12 Version

The ELL Critical Data Process is about gathering the most critical data, getting together the right people (variety of experiences, education, roles, etc.), and using a structured process to have discussions that will help the staff know whether more interventions are needed or if a special education referral is a reasonable option.

Done well, the process helps the team to determine the needed interventions. Or, it helps staff to create the information needed to make a special education referral and to process that referral. It also provides staff with the critical data needed to differentiate between a language learner struggling in the new language and culture, versus a language learner struggling in the new language and culture, who happens to also have a disability.

The ELL Critical Data Process is usually completed as a pre-referral process. However, it can be started after a referral has begun. A referral cannot be delayed solely to complete interventions that were not already completed. However, a team can refuse to propose a special education evaluation if there is other data supporting the need to complete interventions in place of proposing a special education evaluation.

Evaluating the Data from the "Critical Data for ELL Students of Concern" Form

This is a team effort. General education staff, ELL staff, and as appropriate, special education staff, should be involved in the data collection process.

Each of the following factors is provided to allow the team to consider its possible impact on the presenting concern and possible intervention. Each team needs to discuss the extent that they believe these factors impact the child and chart the data on the matrix. The matrix provides a visual with regards to the number and severity of factors that may be impacting the child. The goal is to have the team collect the critical data and have discussions with sufficient depth to understand what the appropriate intervention is for the child (which can include a special education referral).

The team places their marks into the matrix to represent their discussion of each factor, one-at a time. At the end, the matrix represents the result of the team discussion.

Analysis Matrix

FACTORS	1	2	3	4	5	6	7	8	9	10	11	12	13	14	15	16
Data supports referral	■	■														
Between Neutral and Supports Referral	■	■														
Neutral									■			■				
Between Neutral and More Interventions													■			
Data supports more intervention(s)													■			
	1	2	3	4	5	6	7	8	9	10	11	12	13	14	15	16

Red Flag Areas

1. Student's Primary Language
2. Students who speak multiple languages
3. **Red Flag Area** --- Native Language to Primary Language Transition
4. **Red Flag Area** --- Education in Primary/Native Language
5. Parental literacy in primary language
6. Student did not learn to read in the primary language
7. Years learning English
8. Attendance History
9. **Red Flag Area** --- Your Data regarding Your ELL Services --- Results
10. **Red Flag Area** --- Rate of growth on the state language acquisition test
11. **Red Flag Area**--- Intervention Description
12. **Red Flag Area** --- Expectations in the general education classroom
13. Classroom observation
14. Comparison Student Data
15. The parent interview
16. Developmental History

In order to greatly reduce the cost of the printing of this book, and then the cost of purchase for you the reader, we have removed the color content. A large color copy of the matrix is available on the website: stevegillell.com.

Instructions

1) As the team discusses each of the 16 points of data, they need to place a check mark into the appropriate section of the matrix, focusing on each item one at a time, and using the guide to lead their discussions and decisions (e.g., if for factor one the team determined the data supports more intervention(s), place a check mark into the corresponding square for item one).

2) Answer all the items that are easy to answer first (don't just work from 1 to 16 in order). Then, answer the items that take some discussion next, and compromise with the in-between spaces as

needed. Save the items that require more intense discussion until the end, and compromise as needed. The final decision is NOT about a score.

3) Then, analyze the matrix as a whole. That is, do the majority of the check marks appear to be above or below the neutral line (above indicative of a referral and below indicative of more intervention/s)? If it is unclear, discuss the red flag items and use them as a "tie" breaker. This is not about a score, so a single item can be more important than the above/below split if it is a "deal breaker" type item. More explanation to follow.

In the following pages we provide, for each item, its purpose, what information must be gathered, examples of how each item could be rated, and why that item is part of the matrix. The team should have a copy of this section at the meeting in which the matrix is completed.

Examples (these are not rules, just examples!!!)

These examples are meant to provide guidance. There are many other scenarios and possibilities. Use the expertise on the team, the examples, the purpose and the "why" to help guide your team toward the appropriate ratings for each item.

Item number 1: Student's Primary Language

Purpose:

The purpose of this item is to determine whether or not the native language could be directly linked to the struggles the student is having.

Need to know:

First, you need to know the primary/native language of the student. Second, you need to know whether or not the struggles that the student is demonstrating are common or uncommon for students coming from that language to learning English.

Examples:

More Intervention--- The student speaks Spanish or there is a specific example that indicates that the struggles of the student are common for the students coming from the noted language to English.

Neutral--- A student who does not meet the noted criteria above.

Referral --- There are no conditions for item 1 that are indicative of a referral.

Or you may place your mark somewhere in-between based upon your data and discussions.

The Why:

There is research that shows that our students who speak Spanish* are taking more time to acquire English than any other language learner group. This is also the group with the greatest quantity of disproportionality, primarily in the category of Specific Learning Disability. Both of these facts lead to a need to provide more intervention for our Spanish speaking students. In addition, for any student whose problem is a common for students of that language transitioning to English, there is a clear indication of more intervention being needed. **Given that roughly 71-74% of our language learners speak Spanish and given that there will be cases from other languages, this item is rated as "more intervention" about 75% of the time.**

*Discussed later in the book and linked to the need for English. This has nothing to do with the traits of the language Spanish, nor the inherent abilities of the students who speak Spanish. It is all about need for English. The can be true for any of your LTEL (long term English Learner) groups, if the data supports it.

Item Number 2: Students who speak multiple languages

Purpose:

When a student already speaks two or more languages **prior** to learning English and is struggling to learn English, the team needs to examine other possible root problems.

Need to know:

You need to know the languages spoken by the student. If the student speaks only one language, then this item is marked as neutral. You also need to know if there are major life events, like those that could cause trauma, in the history of this student.

Examples:

More Intervention--- The student speaks (and can use) two or more languages and is struggling to learn how to speak English.

Neutral--- Students who speak one language and are learning English.

Referral--- There are no conditions for item 2 that are indicative of a referral.

Or you may place your mark somewhere in between based upon your data and discussions.

The Why:

If a student has shown that they are good at learning languages, given they already speak multiple languages (this should be more than simple conversation, this should be functioning in these languages), the lack of progress as expected in English is probably not related to a potential disability. Therefore, we need to examine other possibilities. This will frequently be neutral, given that multiple languages prior to English is not common. However, this discussion is critical to get the team thinking about trauma, regardless of whether or not there are multiple languages within the home (i.e., multiple languages within the home has no relationship to trauma, trauma just happened to be a strong example of a cause for learning difficulties that is not language acquisition or disability related).

Item number 3: Native language to Primary Language Transition --- Red flag area!

Purpose:

The purpose of this item is to examine language development and transition. This is for students who have enough exposure in the home to multiple languages that they are likely to be learning each language **and** there is evidence they are transitioning from a native language to a primary language. Not all students transition, many become bilingual.

Need to know:

You need to know what languages are spoken in the home. **This item is marked as neutral if only one language is spoken in the home.** For more than one language, you need to know the exposure, experience and expectations with each of the languages.

Examples:

More Intervention--- A student is under the age of 6 and demonstrates difficulties with language development and/or transition across languages*.

Neutral--- A student who is between the ages of 6 and 8, and has difficulties with language development and/or transition across languages. Or, there is only one language in the home.

Referral--- A student who has an environment in which they are likely to develop two or more languages, is over the age of 8, and is demonstrating difficulties with language development and/or transition across languages. This is made stronger if siblings are not demonstrating similar struggles.

Or you may place your mark somewhere in-between based upon your data and discussions.

* Difficulties with language development and/or transition across languages means the student is unsure of which words go with which language. For example, this might be a student who knows red is the correct word when they see something red, but does not know which language red goes with. This same student might know that something is azul when they see something blue, but they don't know which language azul goes with. This student might be able to pick out some of the colors if you ask the questions in Spanish, and other colors when you ask in English. The student might answer at times in

English at times in Spanish. This is contrasted to randomly inserting English words into their Spanish or Spanish words into their English. This could be a lack of vocabulary in one language or the other, and for some students with stronger language skills this could be code switching.

The Why:

If a student has difficulties with language development and/or transition across languages and they are 6-years old or younger, this is normal. Difficulties with language development and/or transition across languages tends to start disappearing between ages 6 and 8, and is abnormal after the age of 8. In all cases, this needs to be judged based upon a student who had a real opportunity to develop the multiple languages. This is powerful when this is the case for the individual student.

Item number 4: Education in native/primary language --- Red flag area!

Purpose:

The purpose of this item is to examine the impact of the student's education in their native language.

This is meant to help the team examine whether or not the student has **transferrable skills.**

Need to know:

You need to know the years of formal education the student has received in their primary/native language. You need to know if they regularly attended school in their native language and appeared to put forth an effort (report cards would be great to see). Last, it would be very helpful to know how their siblings/cousins/peers did in school in their native language.

Examples:

<u>More Intervention</u>--- A student who has not had the **"expected"** years of schooling in their native language.

<u>Neutral</u>--- A student who had the **"expected"** years of schooling in their native language, but the parents indicated attendance was not good in prior setting and the sibling also didn't learn well in that setting.

<u>Referral</u>--- A student who had the **"expected"** years of schooling in their native language, whose siblings learned well in that setting, and this student did poorly compared to siblings/peers.

"Expected" is related to their age. If they are eight, they are "expected" to be in the second grade and therefore have had 2+ years of schooling in their native language. The focus of this item is on transferable skills. The student being born in the US does not make this neutral, the expectation is to help understand the impact of not having transferable skills learned in formal education in their native language.

Or you may place your mark somewhere in-between based upon your data and discussions.

The Why:

A student without formal schooling in their native language is missing transferable skills (e.g., CALP or school specific vocabulary) and understanding school norms (e.g., paying attention to the teacher, going to school every day, using a pencil). Learning these things competes for learning time with whatever else we are trying to teach.

Item number 5: Parental literacy in "primary" language

In this case, this is the language the parent shares with the student; however, the parent might speak multiple languages and is literate in a language they do not use with their child.

Purpose:

The purpose of this item is to examine the exposure of the student to vocabulary and language structures in their native/primary language. Individuals who are not literate in the language they are speaking use a smaller variety of vocabulary, less complex vocabulary, and less complex grammatical structures. Primary language in this case must be the language the parents share with their child, given the relationship of literacy to vocabulary and language structures.

Need to know:

You need to know the literacy level of the parents.

Examples:

Mote Intervention--- A student whose parents are not literate in the language they speak with their child.

Neutral--- A student whose parents have some level of literacy, but indicate reading is difficult for them in the language they speak with their child.

Referral--- A student whose parents are literate in the language they speak with their child.

Or you may place your mark somewhere in-between based upon your data and discussions.

The Why:

The home is the first learning environment. A parent who does not read in the language they speak with their child will use less variety of vocabulary, less complex vocabulary, and less complex grammatical structures. Also, they will not be reading to our student. This puts the student at a competitive disadvantage to other students. Also, it only takes one word per sentence to ruin the understanding. And, achieving these new words in English is more difficult if the student does not know the words in their native language. Again, learning this information will be competing for learning time with whatever we are trying to teach the student. **Do not damage a parent relationship to get this information. More information provider later.**

Item number 6: Student did not learn to read in the primary language

Purpose:

The purpose of this item is to examine the likelihood the student should have learned to read in their native language and the impact of not knowing how to read in the native language on future learning.

Need to know:

You need to know whether or not the student can read at an appropriate level for their exposure, experience, expectations, and practice. Knowing whether or not siblings/cousins/peers learned to read at age-appropriate levels within the same environment is important to know.

Examples:

<u>More Intervention</u>--- A student who did <u>not</u> have an opportunity to learn to read in their native language.

<u>Neutral</u>--- A student who had some opportunity to learn to read in their native language, developed some literacy, but it is unclear the quality of their opportunity as compared to their level of reading development. Or, students who read in their native language.

<u>Referral</u>--- A student whose siblings/peers learned to read with the same exposure/experience/expectations/practice as the student of concern, and the student of concern did not learn to read.

Or you may place your mark somewhere in-between based upon your data and discussions.

The Why:

If the student had a reasonable chance to learn to read, and didn't (but their siblings learned to read in the same environment with the same exposure/experience), this indicates a learning problem for the student. If the student didn't have a reasonable chance of learning to read, we will be trying to teach them to read, in a language they do not fully understand, which will compete with all other learning.

Item number 4 is about educational exposure and experience in native language and item number 6 is reading in native language.

Item number 7: Years learning English

Purpose:

The purpose of this item is to examine the research on how long it takes a student to develop competitive skills when compared to others (based on the research by Cummins, and Collier and Thomas). Also, to counter the belief that a student cannot be evaluated for the possibility of special education services if they have not been learning English for "x" number of years.

Need to know:

You need to know how long they have been learning English formally in our school system.

Examples:

<u>More Intervention</u>--- A student with 0-4 years of learning English.

<u>Neutral</u>--- A student with 4-5 years of learning English.

<u>Referral</u>--- A student with 6-7 (or more) years of learning English

Or you may place your mark somewhere in-between based upon your data and discussions.

*Please note, we don't delay referrals to special education, even one day, for students who are language learners and have a disability that clearly has no relationship to language acquisition (and almost always leads to special education services for our native English speakers), like students who have blindness or deafness.

The Why:

The research shows us that it takes the average language learner 5-7 years to be a competitive learner in our system, when they have a solid ELL program. Therefore, anything less than that puts the student at a competitive disadvantage.

Item number 8: Attendance History

Purpose:

The purpose of this item is to examine why a student is not attending school and the possible interventions to help them want to attend school, and be successful in school.

Need to know:

You need to know their attendance history and how that compares to other students in your school. If their attendance is poor, why are they not attending school? Consider both absences and chronic tardies. You also need to know what "poor" attendance is and have a source for your definition. The early warning system work provides definitions of this.

Examples:

<u>More Intervention</u>--- A student whose attendance is poor for your school, especially a student who has a past history of school success. The student might not be coming to school because school was always easy for them and now it is very difficult for them (they feel defeated and are unsure how to deal with it). Or, a cultural issue that creates a reason for poor attendance.

<u>Neutral</u>--- A student whose attendance is not good but is not notably outside the norm, and there is no documented link between their poor attendance and their school struggles. Or, average attendance.

<u>Referral</u>--- A student with poor school attendance who is not attending school due to a long history of school struggles.

Or you may place your mark somewhere in-between based upon your data and discussions.

The Why:

When a student is not in school, they generally do not learn. Also, their reason for not being in school can be very important to understanding if more intervention or a special education referral is the right option.

Item number 9: Performance of Language Learners in Your Schools --- Red flag area!

Purpose:

The purpose of this item is to determine if the student of concern is a language learner in a system in which language learners in general are finding success, or if the language learners in this setting in general are not finding success.

Need to know:

You need to know how students in your system are doing. This is knowing, not thinking, based upon the test scores and qualification rates of the ELL students in your school when compared to district and state norms. Specific data to know can begin with: percentage of ELLs testing out of state language acquisition levels at/before 5.0 years (or your state cutoff for LTELs), percentage of language learners qualified for special education by district and school (not percentage of special education students who are language learners), and ELL performance on state reading and math testing by language acquisition level.

Examples:

More Intervention--- A student who is doing poorly in a setting in which language learners are in general not doing well compared to state averages is a student who needs more intervention. **This is a systems level problem that needs to be addressed.**

Neutral--- **Do not use neutral for this item.** Use the evidence to take a stance on one side or the other of neutral.

Referral--- A student who is doing poorly in a system in which language learners in general are doing well.

Or you may place your mark somewhere in-between based upon your data and discussions.

The Why:

This allows us to know, not think or believe, we have a student who either is doing poorly when compared to like peers (potential evidence to suspect a disability) or we have a student doing poorly in a system in which language learners in general are doing poorly (casualty of system?).

Item number 10: Rate of growth on the state language acquisition test --- Red flag area!

Purpose:

The purpose of this item is to compare the student against <u>like peers</u> on rate of English language acquisition, as an indicator of learning capacity.

Need to know:

You need to know the language acquisition scores for the student of concern for as many years as is possible and the scores of 3-4 peers who are as similar as possible (language history, country of origin, years learning English, etc.).

Examples:

<u>More Intervention</u>--- The student of concern has the same rate of growth on the state language acquisition tests as the like peers.

<u>Neutral</u>--- The student of concern is **close to** the average performance of like peers.

<u>Referral</u>--- The student of concern is acquiring English at a **much slower** rate than like peers.

Within the next section, the discussion of item 11 covers an easy way to measure "close to" and "much slower." However, this can also be calculated with advanced statistics techniques.

Or you may place your mark somewhere in-between based upon your data and discussions.

The Why:

This data provides us another look at the student's learning capacity along with the other measurable areas, in relationship to like peers.

Item number 11: Intervention Description --- Red flag area!

Purpose:

The purpose of this item is to examine how the student responds to a targeted intervention in comparison to <u>like peers</u>.

Need to know:

You need to know the Response to Intervention for this student and the comparison students to their <u>like peers</u>. This means that your team needed to have designed an appropriately targeted intervention (directed at the area(s) of concern) and delivered it to this student and <u>like peers</u>, and kept ongoing progress data.

Examples:

<u>More Intervention</u>--- The student of concern is responding in a positive manner to the targeted intervention like the other students in the intervention (using <u>like peers</u> for comparison).

<u>Neutral</u>--- The student of concern has growth rates on the targeted intervention that are only slightly lower than those of <u>like peers</u>.

<u>Referral</u>--- The student of concern, when compared to <u>like peers</u>, is responding at a much slower rate to targeted intervention.

Or you may place your mark somewhere in-between based upon your data and discussions.

The Why:

The purpose of this item is to examine how the student responds to a targeted intervention in comparison to <u>like peers</u>. This is a point of data that provides us another look at their learning capacity along with the other measurable areas.

Item number 12: Expectations in the general education classroom --- Red flag area!

Purpose:

The purpose of this item is to understand the impact of the adult expectations on the production and learning of the student.

Need to know:

You need to know the expectations placed upon this student within the general education classroom or classrooms. Use evidence to support this, not just feedback. Evidence would be teachers having work samples that were originally modified for the student's language level, then increased with the growth of the student.

Examples:

<u>More Intervention</u>--- The expectations in the general education classroom(s) were low and there was not a documented system of support for growth.

<u>Neutral</u>--- **Do not use neutral for this item.** Use the evidence to take a stance on one side or the other of neutral.

Referral--- The expectations in the general education classroom matched those normally expected for a student with the same language development level, the student had a system of support (like translanguaging and/or primary language supports), other students responded positively to this, and this student is not responding positively (not demonstrating growth similar to like peers/language learners).

Or you may place your mark somewhere in-between based upon your data and discussions.

The Why:

If the student has not been expected to learn, it is virtually impossible to determine whether or not what we are seeing is a disability (unless we are looking at a low incidence category that we might not need this process for, like students who have blindness or deafness).

Item number 13: Classroom observation

Purpose:

The purpose of this item is to examine the engagement of the student within the classroom setting and relate it to the production and learning of the student.

Need to know:

You need to observe the student and document their participation within the classroom as compared to other like peers, and their levels of success (as related to their apparent effort).

Examples:

More Intervention--- There are no conditions that will lead to a mark below neutral.

Neutral--- A student who is doing little or nothing in the classroom setting.*

Referral--- A student who is trying to follow along with the other students and just is not demonstrating success (in a classroom in which success is the norm).

Or you may place your mark somewhere in-between based upon your data and discussions.

The Why:

This helps us to see if the student is truly putting forth an effort to learn and just is not demonstrating success could be a potential sign of a disability.

*If a student is doing nothing, we do not know if they are doing nothing due to not wanting to do anything, not knowing what they are supposed to be doing (i.e., not understanding the assignment due to language issues) or not knowing what they are supposed to be doing (i.e., a combination of language issues and a possible disability).

Item number 14: Comparison Student Data

Purpose:

The purpose of this item is to find or create any data that can be used to compare the student of concern to peers who are as similar as possible.

Need to know:

Any data you can use to compare this student to other students who are as similar as possible (e.g., ELL students, same language, same language history in English and native language). At the secondary level, this can be the comparison of the student of concern to other language learners in classroom performance across all classes in which there are like peer language learners. Therefore, this could be the most powerful of the items for newcomer secondary students along with targeted intervention data.

Examples:

More Intervention--- Any comparison data* that shows the student learning a skill at the same rate as like peers.

Neutral--- **Avoid using neutral on this item.**

Referral--- Comparison data that shows the student of concern learning at a slower rate than other like peers.

Or you may place your mark somewhere in-between based upon your data and discussions.

*Like science data or this Music/PE example: The Music and/or PE teacher is provided a chart of 4-5 students (who are as similar as possible to the student of concern), and are asked to rate each student on a 1-5 scale. This would occur right after class and the teacher would rate the students from 1 (struggled greatly to learn the new lesson) to 5 (learned the new lesson quickly). The teacher should not know which of the students is the student of concern.

The Why:

This provides us another look at the student's learning capacity, along with the other measurable areas, as compared to like peers.

Item number 15: The parent interview

Purpose:

The purpose of this item is to examine the environment and learning history of the student, siblings, and parents to determine whether or not the student has had the exposure, experience, expectations and practice that are likely to lead to positive learning outcomes. Do not damage or lose a parent relationship to obtain this piece of knowledge. Also, use the staff member who is the best at working with families for the interviewing process.

Need to know:

You need to know about the educational history of the student, their siblings (if they have siblings) and parental educational history.

Example:

More Intervention--- Data that shows there are no developmental issues, parents and siblings learned well, and there are no past issues for this student that are indicative of a potential disability.

Neutral--- **Avoid using neutral on this item.**

Referral--- The data shows a history of learning problems within the family and/or for the student of concern.

Or you may place your mark somewhere in-between based upon your data and discussions.

An example of a single piece of data could be a student from Mexico who has never been in school and who does not speak Spanish, but the school originally thought the student spoke Spanish and kept talking with the student in Spanish. This is a real example and sadly the first district qualified the student as intellectually disabled, doing the testing in Spanish.

The Why:

The team may find information about the environment and learning history of the student, siblings, and parents that completely changes the understanding of the student. This can be used as the totality of data for this item or as a single point of data that can turn the decision-making process one direction or the other.

Item number 16: Developmental History

Purpose:

The purpose of this item is to examine the developmental history, illnesses, and/or injuries of the student of concern to understand if there is something other than language acquisition that would help us to understand the struggles of the student.

Need to know:

You need to know the developmental history of the student (developmental milestones), history of illnesses, medical diagnosis(es), and/or history of injuries.

Example:

More Intervention--- There is no data that indicates health, developmental, or injury issues that could be indicative of a possible disability.

Neutral--- **Avoid using neutral on this item.**

Referral--- The data shows a medical issue(s) likely to be related to a potential disability or a history of poor developmental milestone achievement.

Or you may place your mark somewhere in-between based upon your data and discussions.

An example of a single piece of information could be the parents telling you that in their home country the doctors told them that their child had _____ medical condition, that their child would always struggle to learn, and they have the documents. This is a real example and our team went straight to referral after having the documents translated.

The Why:

Understanding the developmental history, illnesses, and/or injuries of the student of concern can lead to knowing if there is something other than language acquisition that would help us to understand the struggles of the student. This can be used as the totality of data for this item or a single point of data that can turn the decision-making process one direction or the other.

Additional Descriptive Information for some of the items

The following notes are specific to the noted items and are meant to help teams better understand the items as they work through this process. This information is not included above, so that the information above can be used more easily during meetings (i.e., the same format is used for every item above).

Student's Primary Language (1)

As noted earlier, this is rated at more intervention if the student speaks Spanish or if you have a concrete example of the student showing a characteristic/struggle that is common as students transition from their native language to English. This could be a grammar issue that is very common for students who are transitioning from a specific language to English or this could be an articulation issue. Therefore, if you know the students going from language A to English commonly have a certain challenge and this student has the challenge, then more intervention is needed. For many people or districts, these problems are not commonly known. You could go onto a forum/blog of professionals (school psychologist or speech and language pathologist) in your area and ask the question, you could ask people on the executive board for your state association if they know of a resource, and of course you can ask your colleagues in your district. Once you find the answer, work with others in your district to create a resource in which you store this information. The authors of this book have only seen a couple of books on the topic. One of those books is out of print and the other is from England, has some European specific information, and uses the international symbols for sounds that few people know.

The following are two examples to begin the discussion. First, Vietnamese and many other languages have a different prosody than English. In the data sets that I have examined with large populations of students who speak Vietnamese, there has been disproportionate qualification of students who speak Vietnamese under the category of SLI, for articulation. One SLP in my previous setting did extensive research into this area. The characteristics of moving from a language with a distinctly different prosody creates challenges in the new language that are NOT disability related. Therefore, an RTI approach to this would be more appropriate. There are also languages, like German, in which their version of the present tense and the English version of present tense do NOT match up well. Then, students coming from languages like these (e.g., their present tense covers a little bit of the past, the present, and a little bit of the future from an English language perspective) will often struggle with some of the grammar and word usage surrounding concepts of the very recent past and very near future.

Red Flag Area--- Native Language to Primary Language Transition (3)

This item, over the years, has created the most confusion of any item (pun was an accident), because it was called language confusion. Language Confusion has many definitions and not strong agreement. Therefore, the name of this item was changed to reduce the time spent, wasted, on something that isn't core to the item.

Over the years of completing hundreds of evaluations of language learners and consulting on thousands of cases, a pattern became very clear. The vast, vast majority of the difficult cases, cases in which the decision was not clear, were and are students who are transitioning from a native language to a primary language. These are the students whose parents often say, "They kind of understand our language, but they don't speak it." These students have been shown, through research, to have roughly 25% of their vocabulary in their native language, 50% in both languages, and roughly 25% in their new language. When I have tested their vocabulary (Spanish speakers), they almost 100% of the time switch from Spanish to English when the words change from common daily language (BICS) to academic language (CALP). Imagine the struggles these children face in our system. Also, these are the children with the highest rates of overqualification for specific learning disability and the highest rates of being LTELs. This is a systems level problem that must be addressed through backwards mapping to meet the needs of these children and services aligned to meet those needs that are developmentally appropriate at all grade levels, if we want to have different results in the future.

Red Flag Area--- Education in Primary/Native Language (4)

This item is also about structures of language and learned experiences, and the ability to transfer those to the new language and new environment. Consider the following:

A) Knowing that language has specific parts (nouns, verbs etc...) and each language has set patterns in which these occur. This knowledge (or lack thereof) impacts rates of learning.
B) School Experience (norms). If they have not been in school (or don't have the expected number of years), they are learning how to be a student and learning content at the same time. The two compete with each other, which slows the development.
C) Formal Education. Do they know any of the vocabulary of education (e.g., noun, verb, denominator, etc...) from their past experience that they can transfer to their current experience?
D) At this stage, is learning the norms and the language competing with learning to read and do math?

Parental literacy in primary language (5)

This item is focusing on the literacy of the parents and its potential impact upon the child/student. It is critical to note that many languages around the world did not have a written form until the past 50-100 years, and many of those languages have very low rates of literacy due to this fact. There are roughly 7,000 languages on Earth, and there are still approximately 2,000 languages that do not have a written form. Given our acculturation, it is common for people who grew up in the United States (or any country with high literacy rates) to believe that there is a direct relationship between intelligence and literacy. In countries with high literacy rates, there is a correlation. However, many languages have low literacy rates due to having just developed a written form, and some languages still do not have a written form.

Parental literacy – English or not – impacts school preparedness and structure of language. Keep in mind:

A) Worldwide, illiteracy does NOT have a direct correlation with intelligence, especially in countries where education can be difficult to access. In countries with high literacy rates, there can be correlational values.

B) This is to be approached with some caution. That is, some parents will not be comfortable talking about whether or not they are literate. It is very important information to know in order to understand the student's first learning environment – the home. Some staff can obtain this information from the majority of parents without ever upsetting them, some staff struggle to obtain this information or any information. Know your staff and their strengths/challenges.

C) Students who come from homes in which the parents are not literate and/or have limited literacy/education frequently come to school with very limited vocabularies. Studies indicate that the vocabularies of the average kindergartners can/do vary by as much as a factor of 4 (the student with the largest vocabularies have 4 times as many words as those with the lowest vocabularies, and this is NOT including students with disabilities). Is there a "competitive" disadvantage for learning that the student of concern is facing? Not knowing the words in either language is a huge competitive disadvantage!

D) Missing just one word per sentence (vocabulary) can make the sentence meaningless, if it happens to be a key word and a word the student has not yet learned.

Year learning English (7)

This item focuses on the work by Dr. Jim Cummins, and Dr. Virginia Collier and Dr. Wayne Thomas. Dr. Cummins writes about students needing 5-7 years, with ELL services, to be competitive with the native English speakers (he is now qualifying that to students with strong ELL services). Dr. Collier and Dr. Thomas state that it takes a student 6 years in a dual language program (the strongest of programs used in our schools) to perform at the level that represents their "capability." The average for students in this program is above the 50th percentile. This research is often applied inappropriately by teams, saying that a student under 3 or 5 or 7 years (or some other random number) cannot be evaluated for special education services, which is not true, and not appropriate. Students with certain disabilities do not need to wait any length of time (like children with blindness), given that most children with blindness need special education services. In contrast, for children suspected of having a specific learning disability you need much more data to evaluate them correctly (unless you happen to have evidence from their prior country indicative of a learning disability, proof, not guesses or conjecture).

A) The average performance of students who "were" ELL students is still at 32nd-38th percentile, when compared to the group as a whole. So, this is indicating that the students are still at a performance disadvantage which is logical given that speaking a new language and performing in a new language are two distinctly different challenges. "Were" is referring to students who have tested out of eligibility for ELL services.

B) This does not mean no special education testing at all, it means better/more documentation of targeted interventions that are sufficient to help the team know whether or not they are looking at a disability or language learning issue.

C) Better documentation/evidence leads to better decision making.

Attendance History (8)

The key to this item is figuring out why a student is not attending. This helps the team to know whether to design an intervention (and what that might look like) or whether or not they need to move toward a special education referral. Is a student not attending because school was always easy for them and it is suddenly hard, are they not attending because in their culture school is optional, are they not attending school because they have always struggled in school, so why attend?

Poor attendance is a high predictor of dropout rate.

Bench press 400 pounds each day story: "If I were to take you into the gym each day and place 400 pounds on the bench press and you had to try it, how long would it take you to be avoidant? How unpleasant would this be for you? Some of our students experience this when asked to come to school and they naturally want to avoid the painful and unsuccessful experience." What can we do to alleviate this?

It is important to take the time to investigate a source regarding what is "poor" attendance. I usually search the literature on "early warning systems." This provides information regarding when attendance is likely to predict school failure and/or drop out.

Red Flag Area--- Your Data Regarding Your ELL Services --- Results (9)

This item was changed to put the primary focus on data. Are the language learners in your setting successful when compared to language learners in other buildings within your district, to other districts, and to the state data? This is crucial to know whether you are looking at a student who is not having success within a system in which most of the language learners are finding success (possible indicator to suspect a disability). In contrast, are you looking at a student who is not having success within a system where language learners in general are not having success (possible casualty of the system that isn't working for language learners)?

Additionally, the research by Dr. Virginia Collier and Dr. Wayne Thomas (google the Thomas and Collier graph) is based on over 7,000,000 student files. This research clearly shows that dual language programs have far superior results, especially when compared to the most common model, pull-out services.

There are times, though, that star teachers can overcome the odds that are stacked against the program models that are not known to be successful models. This needs to be documented with proof. For example, if you have an ELL teacher/program that you believe is beating the odds (e.g., a pull-out model that is working), you need to be able to produce data like the following: the students are making it through the language acquisition levels faster than is the local and state norm, the students are scoring higher on the local and state testing than is the state norm, your school has a lower percentage of LTELs, your school has a lower than average rate of qualifying language learners for special education. Then, if you have a student who is doing poorly in this program model, you have evidence of a student who might have difficulties learning (as long as there is not another reason that you know could or would explain the difficulties).

Red Flag Area--- Intervention Description (11)

In order to accurately evaluate a language learner for one of the "soft" disability categories, like SLD, SLI or DD, who has not been learning English for the 5-7 years, you should* have delivered a targeted invention to this student and a group of like peers. Then, if this student does not respond to the intervention in a manner similar to that of like peers, you have evidence that could support the possibility of a disability.

Intervention is TARGETED. But, how do you know that your intervention is what the child actually needs?

A) Reading is a major and extremely common component of most special education referrals, but reading has 5 (or more depending upon your training) key areas: sight words, phonics/phonemes, fluency, vocabulary, and comprehension. Have you done what you need to do to know which area(s) need the intervention? If a student has problems with letter sounds, do you know whether or not those sounds exist in their L1?

B) During interventions, you need comparison students who are similar (language, school history, etc) to compare growth rates (see the charts on the following pages). Also, note that data monitoring must be completed on an ongoing basis so that one data point (beginning or end) cannot destroy the meaning.

*A referral and/or evaluation for special education services cannot be delayed or refused solely based upon the lack of interventions prior to that point in time. In other words, in order to process a special education referral and refuse to evaluate, the team needs more data than the simple fact that interventions had not already been tried and shown to not be sufficient. For example, if a student has blindness your team would not be expected to attempt an intervention prior to proposing a special education evaluation.

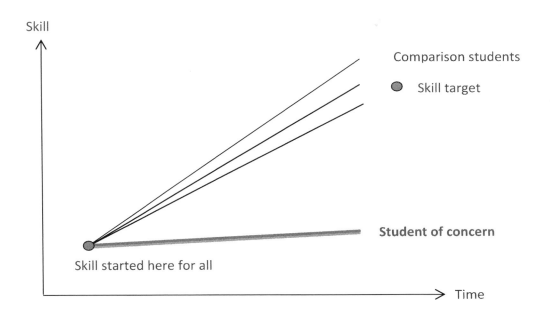

If a targeted intervention was delivered and the graph has an appearance similar to this, then you are looking at evidence that is indicative of a referral for a possible special education evaluation. Use ongoing measurement of data.

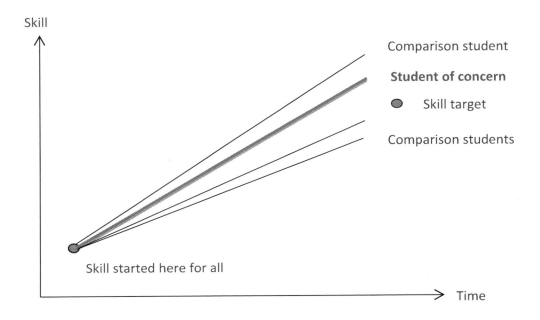

If a targeted intervention was delivered and the graph has an appearance similar to this, you are looking at a student who just needs (in all likelihood) more targeted intervention. Use ongoing measurement of data.

This is the perfect place to discuss the concept of "a little lower" or "significantly" lower than like peers. Imagine this same graph (the one with all students near the skill target), but the student of concern is the lowest student. Your job would be to calculate the average difference of the scores of the four students and determine whether or not the student of concern was less, equal, or farther below the next student above them. For example, if the four students have scores of 100, 95, 90, and 85 the average difference would be 5 points. Then, the lowest of these four students is only slightly lower than the other students and this score might actually represent strong performance on the intervention (something to discuss). In contrast, if the scores were 100, 95, 90, and 70, there would be a significant difference between the third and fourth student and the lowest score might be representing poor performance on the intervention.

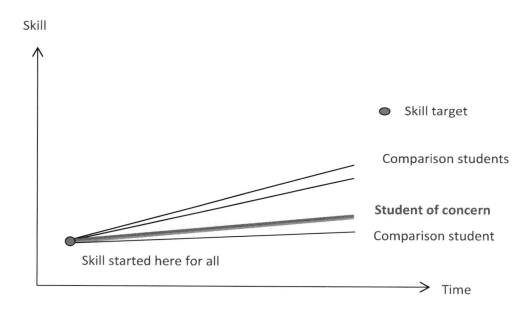

If a targeted intervention was delivered and the graph has an appearance similar to this, then you are looking at a problem with curriculum, instruction quality or both. Use ongoing measurement of data.

No quantity of the wrong intervention will fix the actual need!

Red Flag Area--- Expectations in the general education classroom (12)

We need to know that the student of concern had reasonable expectations and a support system to achieve reasonable results. The students need to have the expectation to complete work like other students from day 1. If they can only draw a picture on day one, that is fine. Then, move to labeling the pictures, then to writing short sentences, etc...

Bench Press example continued from earlier: Earlier we described how unlikely it would be for someone (an average person) to try to bench press 400 pounds and want to try that again each day, given it is highly likely that their attempts would lead to a great deal of pain. What if someone helped them determine what their 80% of maximum bench press was, gave them a program of practice in sets of 10 at the appropriate weight, and the weight was increased each time sets of 10 became "easy?" Then we would see their ability to grow the skill in comparison to like peers.

It is all about meeting someone at their skill/ability/developmental level and providing the opportunity for them to grow and the path on which they can travel to make the growth. If in the end, they do not make growth like other students when the other students are provided a similar experience, then we have evidence of a possible need to make a referral. In contrast, if they make average levels of growth, then we know that we need to keep having reasonable/appropriate expectations (while we provide supports). This can make staff uncomfortable. Focus on the evidence. That is, instead of asking people whether or not they are providing appropriate expectations and appropriate support, ask them to provide the team evidence that supports this is occurring.

Classroom observation (13)

We are trying to see the effort level and engagement of the student within the general education setting. If they are not engaged and not trying to achieve, we really cannot draw any conclusions for this item. That is, a student who is doing nothing tells us nothing. They may not be doing anything because they don't know what to do. They may not know what to do because they do not have strong enough language skills or we are not doing what is necessary to make the content comprehensible. They may not be doing anything because they have a cognitive disability and cannot understand the concepts or steps involved. We just do not know, if they are not doing anything. In contrast, a student in a well-run classroom who is trying to do the lesson, who is watching their peers, and still is not having success is a student who may have a disability, and a special education referral may be appropriate for this student.

At middle school and high school, we are guaranteed a well-run classroom (given in elementary we don't get to choose from 6 teachers where the observation will occur, and middle/high school we do have this choice). There will be times at elementary in which the student is in a classroom that is not well-run. If this is the case, the first thing an observer can do, if they do not know what the student looks like, is to observe in the classroom and see if they can pick 3 students (with the student of concern being one of those 3 students). If they cannot, then there are other problems that need to be addressed. If they can, they need to return on another day, pick two other students (in addition to the student of concern) and observe all three. If the other students are chosen at random and the student of concern does not appear notably different than these students, there are other problems that need to be addressed.

This is all about making sure there isn't another reason for what you are seeing as the presenting concerns and/or learning what needs to be addressed via intervention.

Developmental History (16)

When working with parents, we need to take caution and check for meaning when certain key words are used, like noted below. Also, if we are having the parents or teachers complete any type of rating scale, we need to guard against the impacts of frustration, anger, guilt, denial, etc.

A) Use caution with parent statements of things like normal or slow, make sure to ask questions to understand what they are expressing. Parents whose other children are all in highly capable student programs (except this student) would possibly call the student in question slow even though they are "normal" and parents who have children with disabilities may call a student with obvious issues normal.
B) Remember the rules of thirds when staff or parents are describing traits - 1/3 are too "harsh" in their ratings (anger, frustration, guilt, etc...), 1/3 are pretty accurate, 1/3 are too "soft or hesitant" in their ratings (denial, fear, etc...). This is Steve's personal opinion based on many years of completing evaluations.

Steve had a teacher and both parents complete a behavioral rating scale for a student a few years ago, and received very unusual results. The student had 12 of the 14 areas rated as clinically significant for problem behaviors and 6 of the 7 areas rated as clinically significant for prosocial behaviors (meaning a lack of prosocial skills/abilities). The ratings were very consistent and very severe. However, the worst behaviors that the student was demonstrating were reading his choice book at inappropriate times and taking too many bathroom breaks. The people were very frustrated with this student, and their ratings did not represent the observable behaviors.

Appendix C (first half for K-12 Version) provides information regarding using the data to design interventions or support either a special education referral or special education evaluation.

Data Collection Example Form for Critical Data Process - K-12 Version

The following is an example of a data collection form used to gather the data. This can easily be turned into a fillable document by any individual well trained in Microsoft products or Google Docs. It is critical that a team (3-5 staff members) gather the data. With a smaller team, staff members may be overwhelmed by their overall work duties and may not have the necessary time to devote to this process. A school team can divide the work in quite a variety of ways, the important factor being that it works for those involved and the best data possible is gathered.

In the end, life changing decisions will be made based upon the data that is gathered. Better data leads to a higher likelihood that appropriate decisions are being made for the student.

On the following pages is a sample of a form, or a beginning to a form, for collected data. Over the years, I have found that people find their data collection forms to be very personal. So, take this just as a starting point and change it as you would like (not the ELL Critical Data Items or process, but how you collect your data).

Critical Data for ELL Students of Concern

Data Collection Form

Student Name: _____

Birthdate: _____

Date: _____

Primary concern(s) noted by staff or parent(s):

_____

_____

_____

Student's Primary/Native language: _____

Other languages spoken by student and their usage: _____

_____

Language(s)spoken in the home: _____

Years of formal education in primary/native language: _____

How did siblings or relatives learn and/or perform in that environment: _____

_____

Parental literacy in language spoken with child: _____

_____

Can student read/write in primary/native language: Yes/No

If yes, at what level can they read or write in primary language: _____

How well did sibling and/or relatives learn to read in that environment: _____

_____

_____

Exposure/Experience/Expectations/Practice related to reading instruction:

_____

_____

_____

Number of years learning English: _____

Attendance History (if poor, explain why):

_____

_____

ELL Student Performance Data/Evidence (school versus district versus state):

_____

_____

_____

State Language Acquisition test data (including number of years at each level). Include test scores for this student and 3-4 like peers:

_____

_____

_____

Interventions description (describe intervention, including pre, ongoing, and post test data and length of intervention and include the data of the comparison students who are like peers):

_____

_____

_____

Expectations while in general education classroom (e.g., was student expected to turn in class work and homework every time other students were (albeit modified)). How were the expectations supported?

Were these expectations of skills development/language development level appropriate? If no/none/limited evidence is needed. How are other ELL students doing in this/these classes?

_____

_____

_____

_____

Classroom observation (and completed by), comparison student behavior (engaged in learning, on-task, how determined):

_____

_____

_____

_____

_____

_____

Current academic levels in English. How does that look when viewed through the LE³AP lens?

_____

Comparison student data (describe the measurement and how like peers did on same measurement):

_____

_____

_____

_____

(To complete this section, you need at least 3 students whose language background is similar to the student of concern and for whom you have the same type of classroom or standardized test data. The core question is: how does the development of the student of concern compare/contrast to other students with very similar language backgrounds?).

Information gained primarily during Parent Interview

Academic history/performance in primary language (should include, but is not limited to: age when student started school, average age when students start school in their country, performance in school, retention, highest grade level studied, any difficulties in native and/or primary language, family history of learning experiences, behavioral norms for children):

_____

_____

_____

_____

_____

_____

Academic performance compared to siblings/peers:

_____

_____

_____

_____

Developmental and medical history (questions can include, but are not limited to: age student began to walk, began to talk, recognized own name written, wrote own name, gross motor skills compared to peers, fine motor skills compared to peers, peer interactions, illnesses, injuries):

_____

_____

_____

_____

_____

_____

Chapter 4: ELL CDP Mini-Matrix

Specific Learning Disability and ELL Students with less than 5-7 years learning English

The descriptions below show how the data for these items can support eligibility for special education services, be neutral on the issue, or contradict eligibility for special education services. If the team has parent permission to evaluate a language learner and there is a possibility of a specific learning disability, these items and this information needs to be carefully considered and documented.

Please note, this information is not as useful if the team does not know their data on their usage of SLD as a category for all students versus language learners, and do not know the success rate of ELL students within the school and district (e.g., rates of language acquisition, test scores on local, state and national tests, graduation rates).

Strong performance in general of the ELLs, and a student who is doing very poorly, indicates an individual student problem. In contrast, poor performance of ELL students in general makes it much more difficult to separate ELLs with disabilities from students who are casualties of a system that does not work well for students in general. Therefore, your decision-making power gets stronger if your data proves that you have a system in which language learners are not overqualified in general and are having success in general (based upon data/proof). Your decision-making power gets weaker as your data shows over qualification and/or poor performance of ELL students in general (poor language acquisition, poor general test scores).

There are more items below regarding supporting eligibility given that most students who are considered for a special education referral should not reach the stage of a special education evaluation unless there is already supporting data that a special education evaluation is needed. Therefore, if you don't see many of these, your case for potential eligibility is not as strong.

NOTE: Some of the descriptions/examples for the CDP Mini-Matrix are much different than those provided for the ELL Critical Data Process, given that that the earlier examples are related to intervention versus referral and this section is about whether or not the evidence supports or does not support a disability.

Names of the items, by number, from the ELL Critical Data Process

1. Student's Primary Language
2. Students who speak multiple languages
3. **Red Flag Area** --- Native Language to Primary Language Transition
4. **Red Flag Area**--- Education in Primary/Native Language
5. Parental literacy in primary language
6. Student did not learn to read in the primary language
7. Years learning English
8. Attendance History

9. **Red Flag Area** --- Your data regarding your language learners --- Results
10. **Red Flag Area**--- Rate of growth on the state language acquisition test
11. **Red Flag Area**--- Intervention Description
12. **Red Flag Area** --- Expectations in the general education classroom
13. Classroom observation
14. Comparison Student Data
15. The parent interview
16. Developmental History

Not all items are included in the examples that follow, given that not all of the items affect the decision-making process for the possibility of a specific learning disability.

Items from the ELL Critical Data Process and examples in which Specific Learning Disability is <u>not supported</u> by the information gathered:

Item 3 (Native Language to Primary Language Transition): If the student is within this group and your districts has disproportionality within this group, then a great deal of other data is needed to overcome this fact in support of eligibility.

Item 4 (Education in primary/native language): If there is evidence of formal education in primary language and average to above average performance, this is data indicating that they do not have a learning disability.

Item 6 (Student did not learn to read in the native/primary language): If the student of concern learned to read in their native language (at a level commensurate with their exposure, experience, expectations and practice), this is data indicating that they do not have a learning disability.

Item 8 (Attendance history): If the student of concern is not attending school in the US, because in their country they were successful in school and they are not successful here in the US (i.e., avoiding school in this new setting because they are not having success like in the past or a cultural issue is noted), this is data indicating that they do not have a learning disability.

Item 10 (Rate of growth on the state language acquisition test): If the student of concern is learning English at the same rate as their like peers, this is data indicating that they do not have a learning disability.

Item 11 (Intervention description): If the student of concern responds positively to targeted intervention, at a level similar to or higher than like peers, this is data indicating that they do not have a learning disability.

Item 14 (Comparison student data): If there is another source of data used to compare the student of concern against like peers for rate of learning, and the student of concern scores in a similar manner to that of like peers, this is data indicating that they do not have a learning disability.

Item 15 (Parent interview): If there is no past evidence of learning problems for the student of concern, nor within the family, this is data indicating that they do not have a learning disability.

Item 16 (Developmental history): All or almost all developmental milestones were met at expected times. This indicates normal development and is not supportive of the likelihood of a disability (not a powerful item for SLD).

Items from the ELL Critical Data Process and examples in which Specific Learning Disability is neutral by the information gathered:

Item 4 (Education in primary/native language): If there is evidence that the student of concern did poorly during education in their primary language, but the system is known to have inconsistent levels of success for students, then this evidence is neutral (does not help during the evaluation process), regarding SLD.

Item 6 (Student did not learn to read in the native/primary language): If the student of concern did not have a reasonable opportunity to learn to read in their native language, and didn't learn to read in their native language, then this evidence is neutral (does not help during the evaluation process), regarding SLD.

Item 11 (Intervention description): If the student of concern is receiving a targeted intervention and their performance is only slightly lower than that of like peers, then this evidence is neutral (does not help during the evaluation process), regarding SLD.

Item 13 (Classroom observation): If the student of concern is not appearing engaged in the classroom, then this evidence is neutral (does not help during the evaluation process), regarding SLD.

Item 14 (Comparison student data): If there is another source of data used to compare the student of concern against like peers for rate of learning, and the student of concern scores are **slightly lower*** than those of like peers, then this evidence is neutral (does not help during the evaluation process), regarding SLD.

*determining slightly lower and significantly lower is explained in the section for additional information on the ELL Critical Data Process K-12 Version

Items from the ELL Critical Data Process and examples in which Specific Learning Disability is supported by the information gathered:

Item 3 (Native Language to Primary Language Transition): If the student of concern is showing struggles with language development and transition, has had targeted interventions that have been proven to work with other students within your setting, and they are responding much slower, then this is evidence toward eligibility.

Item 4 (Education in primary/native language): If there is evidence that the student of concern had formal education in their native language and they did poorly (when peers and/or siblings did well), then this is supportive data for the possibility of a learning disability (this becomes stronger as the student of concern is more unlike peers and/or siblings in the same environment).

Item 5 (Parental literacy in primary language): If the parents of the student of concern are highly literate in the commonly used language (language spoken between parents and child), and they read to the student of concern in this language, and this student is doing poorly in school, then this is evidence that supports the possibility of a learning disability.

Item 6 (Student did not learn to read in the native/primary language): If the student of concern had a strong opportunity to learn to read in their native language (peers and/or siblings learned to read in the same environment), and the student of concern did not learn to read, then this is evidence that supports the possibility of a learning disability.

Item 8 (Attendance history): If the student of concern is not attending school because they have a history of doing poorly in school (peers and/or siblings normally did well in the same environment), then this is evidence that supports the possibility of a learning disability.

Item 9 (Your data for your language learners --- Results): If the student is in a setting in which language learners are successful, based upon measurable data, and they are not demonstrating success, then this supports the possibility of a learning disability. This is stronger and stronger as the student is more unlike their language learning peers (i.e., if this is the only language learner having learning difficulties, this would be very strong data).

Item 10 (Rate of growth on the state language acquisition test): If the student of concern is acquiring English at a much slower rate than their like peers in your school, based on state language acquisition testing, then this is evidence that supports the possibility of a learning disability.

Item 11 (Intervention description): If the student of concern is responding to targeted intervention at a **much slower rate*** than like peers, then this is evidence that supports the possibility of a learning disability.

*determining slightly lower and significantly lower is explained on in the section for additional information on the ELL Critical Data Process K-12 Version

Item 12 (Expectations in the general education classroom): If the student of concern is in an environment in which there are strong expectations that are supported by a system of support (evidence is needed to prove this, not opinion), and the student is doing poorly, then this is evidence that supports the possibility of a learning disability. This is stronger if the other language learners in the environment/classroom are doing well.

Item 13 (Classroom observation): If the student of concern is in a well-run classroom, and they are engaged in the learning (e.g., they watch peers and teachers then try to mimic or copy what they are doing), and this student is producing very low-quality work (in comparison to like peers), and the quality is not improving, then this is evidence that supports the possibility of a learning disability. This is stronger if the other language learners in the environment/classroom are doing well.

Item 14 (Comparison student data): If the student of concern is shown to score much lower than like peers on measurable data, then this is evidence that supports the possibility of a learning disability. (This is not reading, math or written language, given those should be addressed in the targeted interventions).

Item 15 (The parent interview): If the parents report that the student of concern has always struggled with learning (and/or have report cards from the previous environment) and those struggles match the struggles that the team is seeing in the current environment, then this is evidence that supports the possibility of a learning disability.

Item 16 (Developmental History): All developmental milestones are low.

For each of these examples, you can take what is written above and make minor modifications to use within your evaluation report to address whether or not language learning or language learning with a disability is the determinant factor. The following are examples of this. And, you would need to do the same for each of the items in which there are meaningful results.

An example for using an item as one of the pieces of data within the report to indicate a student **is not** eligible for special education as a student with a learning disability:

Statement from above:

Item 11: If the student responds positively to targeted intervention, at or higher than like peers, this is data indicating that they do not have a learning disability.

What you could write:

Jose was involved in a targeted intervention to address concerns regarding his skills in reading vocabulary. This area was targeted for intervention given that he was found to be in the lowest 10% of the fourth-grade students in this area. When Jose was compared to like peers (other ELL students who speak Spanish and have been learning English for 3 years), his rate of growth during the intervention was within the average for the group. Therefore, this is evidence to indicate that Jose does not have a Specific Learning Disability.

An example for using an item as one of the pieces of data within the report to indicate a student **is** eligible for special education as a student with a learning disability:

Statement from above:

Item 11: If the student of concern is responding to targeted intervention at a much slower rate than like peers, then this is evidence that supports the possibility of a learning disability.

What you could write:

Jose was involved in a targeted intervention to address concerns regarding his skills in reading vocabulary. This area was targeted for intervention given that he was found to be in the lowest 10% of the fourth-grade students in this area. When Jose was compared to like peers (other ELL students who speak Spanish and have been learning English for 3 years), his rate of growth during the intervention was significantly lower than that of his peers. When this piece of data is combined with _____ (your other supporting data), this is evidence that learning English is not the determinant factor with regards to the delayed development Jose is demonstrating, but instead that Jose has a specific learning disability in addition to being a language learner. The combination of the evidence indicates that Jose would demonstrate this disability regardless of whether or not he was a language learner.

Throughout this book, and our book *Evaluating ELL Students for the Possibility of Special Education Qualification- Second Edition*, you will find more examples of written content for reports as related to these items. Also, our workbook *The ELL Special Education Evaluation Workbook*, that is a partner book to this book *The ELL Critical Data Process,* is an entire example of integrating the concepts of this book.

The SLD Mini-Matrix

Analysis matrix for suspicion of SLD in language learners with less than 5 years learning English

FACTORS	3	4	5	6	8	9	10	11	12	13	14	15
Data supports SLD qualification												
Neutral												
Data does not support SLD qualification												
	3	4	5	6	8	9	10	11	12	13	14	15

The matrix you will be working with when completing the ELL Critical Data Process will have the red-flag areas highlighted in red and the neutral row highlighted in green (in order to reduce the cost printing of this book we are providing you the matrix without the color coding). Also, this matrix does not use all of the factors/numbers, because not all of them provide information regarding SLD for language learners with less than 5 years learning English.

After you have filled out the mini-Matrix, are there mostly marks in "neutral" and "Data supports SLD qualification?" Then the evidence is likely to be supportive of a special education qualification, knowing the work has been completed across the ELL Critical Data Process, school/district data analysis, and the special education evaluation.

Any marks in the "Data does not support SLD qualification" section should be carefully examined and discussed before moving forward. Anything that brings into question the decision to qualify a language learner as a student with a specific learning disability must be examined and explained so that a stranger to the student can understand what decision was made, what data the decision was based upon, and that the decision appears logical given the data. If you under qualified ELL students in your district, based on your data, the logic would be reversed. Examine and know your data to make sure your team is using facts to guide decisions.

Chapter 5: ELL Critical Data Process - Preschool Version

The Preschool Version of the ELL Critical Data Process takes staff through a process of examining the exposure, experience, expectations and practice that the child has had regarding the skill or behavior in question. This focuses on issues that could be related to a potential disability in the areas of speech/language and/or developmental delays.

Children with profound disabilities are highly likely to need special education services, regardless of their language development in English. Also, disproportionality is most prevalent in the categories of Speech or Language Impairment, Developmental Delay, and Specific Learning Disability. Only the first two are possible (in most states) for our preschool age students, given that the category of Specific Learning Disability often starts at first grade.

There is rarely measurable data with children at this age, therefore we need to utilize the information we have available to us and compare the child of concern against children (who are true like peers) who have developed the skill or behavior that the child of concern is struggling to develop.

As with the K-12 version, this is a team process. Multiple team members must be involved in the data collection process and data processing.

Each of the following factors is provided to allow the team to consider the possible impact on the presenting concern and possible intervention. Each team is to discuss the extent that they believe these factors impact the child and chart the data on the provided matrix. The matrix provides a visual with regards to the number and severity of factors that may be impacting the child. The goal is to have the team collect the critical data and have discussions with sufficient depth to understand what the appropriate intervention is for the child (which can include a special education referral).

The following numbers correspond to the numbers on the matrix. The team places their marks into the matrix to represent their discussion of each factor, one at a time. The completed matrix represents the result of the team discussion.

Important Note: It is critical to understand the child's environment and experience (exposure to experiences and language/s) in order to have meaningful discussions.

Layout of this section:

First, you will see the matrix with the list of items. Then, for each item, we provide you with the purpose of the item, information needed to be gathered (in general, you might find you need more for a specific child), examples for each item related to how to rate the item, then the "Why" of each item. Last, further information is provided for each item.

Analysis Matrix

FACTORS	1	2	3	4	5	6	7	8	9 A	9 B
Data supports referral										
Between Neutral and Supports Referral										
Neutral										
Between Neutral and More Interventions										
Data supports more intervention(s)										
	1	2	3	4	5	6	7	8	9 A	9 B

1. Exposure
2. Experience
3. Expectations in the household/daycare
4. Intervention (Practice) description
5. Parental literacy in primary language
6. Approach taken with regards to English learning
7. Child's primary language, environment, and need to learn English
8. Observation
9A. The parent interview
9B. Developmental history

In order to greatly reduce the cost of the printing of this book, and then the cost of purchase for the reader, we have removed the color content. A large color copy of the matrix is available on the website: stevegillell.com.

Instructions

1) As the team discusses each of the 10 points of data, they need to place a check mark into the appropriate section of the matrix (e.g., if for factor one the team determined the data supports more intervention(s), place a check mark into the corresponding square).

2) Answer all the items that area easy to answer first (don't just work from 1 to 9B in order). Then, answer the items that take some discussion and compromise with the in-between spaces as needed. Save the items that require more intense discussion until the end, and compromise as needed. The final decision is NOT about a score.

3) Then, analyze the matrix as a whole. That is, do the majority of the check marks appear to be above or below the neutral line (above supporting a referral and below supporting more intervention/s)? If it is unclear, then planning targeted intervention is likely to be the appropriate decision, given that special education is about a disability that creates an adverse impact and the need for specially designed instruction. Also, our qualification data clearly demonstrates over qualification.

4) This is NOT about a score, but is instead about letting the discussions lead the team to understanding what a child needs via following a structured process. That is, the number above or below could be indicative of a referral or more intervention, but the team can conclude otherwise based upon the quality and depth of their discussions. The goal is the ability to choose the most appropriate next steps for each child based upon data.

The following examples are to assist, but not to limit. These are not rules, but guidelines.

It is critical that all comparison children are like peers, children who come from the same language and cultural background. Special Note: the students who come from languages that are rare within your district are like peers for one another.

Exposure (1):

Purpose:

The purpose of this item is to determine the level of exposure the child has had to the skill or behavior of concern, then to compare that level of exposure to children who have gained the skill or behavior.

Information Needed:

The team needs to gather data regarding the exposure the child has had to each of the skill areas or behaviors that are concerning the team.

Examples:

More Intervention: If the child has not had the same exposure to the skill area as children who have developed the skill to the expected level, then the mark should be made toward more intervention.

Neutral: The child has been exposed to the skill or behavior of concern, but the parent reports are unclear on the quality of the exposure.

Referral: If the child has had the expected level of exposure, similar to children who have gained the skills, and the child of concern is still not demonstrating the skills, then the mark should be made in the matrix toward referral.

Or place the mark somewhere in-between based upon your data and discussions.

The Why:

In order to understand whether or not the skill or behavior of concern represents a lack of exposure or a potential disability, the child's exposure to the skill or behavior has to be examined in contrast to children who have developed the skill or behavior.

Experience (2):

Purpose:

The team is trying to compare the experiences the child had with the skill of concern against the experiences of children who are doing well developing the same skill. Exposure is simply contact with something and experience is involvement with the same thing, or direct participation.

Information Needed:

The team needs to gather data regarding the experience the child has had with each of the skill areas or behaviors that are concerning the team.

Examples:

More Intervention: If the child of concern did not actively participate in the activities as did the children who gained the skill(s), then mark toward more intervention.

Neutral: The child has experience with the skill or behavior of concern, but the parent reports are unclear on the quality of the experience.

Referral: If the child directly participated in the activities needed to gain the skill(s) at the same level as children who commonly gain the skills, and the child of concern didn't gain the skills, then mark toward referral.

Or place the mark somewhere in-between based upon your data and discussions.

The Why:

In order to understand whether or not the skill or behavior of concern represents a lack of experience or a potential disability, the child's experience with the skill or behavior has to be examined in contrast to children who have developed the skill or behavior.

Expectations in the household/daycare (3):

Purpose:

This is to understand what expectations have been placed on the child by the adults within their life (parents, siblings, daycare providers, etc.). **Is the desired skill or behavior developmentally appropriate? Developmentally appropriate within the culture of the student? How do you know?**

Information Needed:

Is the child attempting to make their needs known, and how? How do adults respond? Are adults allowing the child to become frustrated at times?

Is the child attempting daily tasks? Examples? How do adults respond? Are the adults allowing the child to become frustrated at times?

Has the child received a different set of expectations than he/she is currently facing? Do the new environment and previous environment expectations match? Has there been a major change in the family that created different, new expectations?

What are the behavioral expectations placed on the child? How is the child reinforced? How is the child given consequences?

Was the environment such that the skill (that may be in question) was needed? Was there an opportunity to practice the skill?

How are your (the staff member's) personal biases/expectations impacting reviewing the situation?

Examples:

More Intervention: A child who is producing very little language that can be understood outside immediate family, and the caretakers try to meet the needs of the child, with no efforts or strategy to improve the communication. The child does not use language, the language might not be needed to get their needs met. Or, it might be that the child has a potential disability. A targeted intervention is needed to determine which one of these is the likely scenario.

Neutral: A child who is difficult to understand by strangers, family/caretakers make some efforts to encourage speech production and some efforts to correct, but the efforts are inconsistent.

Referral: An example is: 1) A child who is producing very little language that can be understood outside the immediate family, 2) and the family has tried to work with the child over a long period of time to mimic the sounds/words and encourages the child to make approximations of the correct words (to get their needs met), 3) but there is very little change in speech/communication skills. The adult behaviors indicate the expectations (i.e., Are the adults over functioning for the child to avoid tantrums?)

Or place the mark somewhere in-between based upon your data and discussions.

The Why:

We need to know whether the skill or behavior of concern was expected by the people in the child's world, worked on to improve by the people in the child's world, and reinforced for improvement in order to know whether or not the deficit presents like a possible disability or presents like a lack of exposure/experience/expectations/practice. **Is the desired skill or behavior developmentally appropriate? Developmentally appropriate within the culture of the student? How do you know?**

For item number 3 the focus is on the parent, sibling, teacher, care provider expecting the child to do the behavior/skill and for item number 4 the focus is on what system of practice/intervention is in place to help the child improve the behavior/skill. And, the quality, fidelity, and age/developmental appropriateness of the practice/intervention.

Intervention (Practice) Description (4):

Purpose:

To understand what efforts have been made to improve the skill or behavior in question.

Information Needed:

Describe the concern after discussion and review with the team. Be as concrete as possible (e.g., "doesn't comply" is not specific, "when asked to put on his shoes he lays on the ground and screams" is specific).

Was the child's environment such that they needed the skills? Was the child's environment supportive of developing those skills?

What specifically has been done to address the concern? What were the results? What was the frequency and duration of the intervention? **Is the desired skill or behavior developmentally appropriate? Developmentally appropriate within the culture of the student? How do you know?**

Examples:

More Intervention: There is little or no evidence of a systematic effort over time to teach the child the skill (or a new skill to replace the undesired behavior).

Neutral: There were efforts to work with the child in order to change the behavior or teach a new skill, but the efforts were not consistent (lacked fidelity) and the intervention was not very long (less than 8-10 weeks).

Referral: There is evidence of an intervention that was targeted to teach a new skill or replacement behavior in order to address the concern noted, it was delivered with fidelity for more than 8 weeks, and the child made little or no progress.

Or place the mark somewhere in-between based upon your data and discussions.

The Why:

We need to know whether the skill or behavior of concern was expected by the people in the child's world. Then, we need to know the quality, fidelity, and age/developmental appropriateness. Is the desired skill or behavior developmentally appropriate? Developmentally appropriate within the culture of the student? How do you know? Without this, it is impossible to know whether the student is struggling to learn (i.e., possible disability) or if they don't have an environment that supports the desired learning per the expectations of this new environment.

Parental literacy in "primary" language (5):

Purpose:

The purpose of this item is to examine the exposure of the child to vocabulary and language structures in **the language the parents share with the child (i.e., the parents might be literate in a language they do not share with the child).** Individuals who are not literate in the language they are speaking use a smaller variety of vocabulary, less complex vocabulary, and less complex grammatical structures.

Need to know:

You need to know the literacy level of the parents in the language they share with their child.

Example:

More Intervention: A child whose parents are not literate in the language they share with the child.

Neutral: A child whose parents have some level of literacy in shared language, but indicate reading is difficult for them in the language they share with the child.

Referral: A child whose parents are literate in the language they share with the child.

Or place the mark somewhere in-between based upon your data and discussions.

The Why:

The home is the first learning environment. A parent who does not read in the language they share with the child will use less variety of vocabulary, less complex vocabulary, and less complex grammatical structures. Also, they will not be reading to their child in the shared language. This puts the child at a competitive disadvantage to other children. Also, it only takes one word per sentence to ruin the understanding. And, achieving these new words in English is more difficult if the child does not know the words in their native language. Again, learning this information will be competing for learning time with whatever we are trying to teach the child.

Approach taken with regards to English learning (6):

Purpose:

If the child is speaking English, even if only a little, we can use this to understand how well they learn in comparison to their siblings and their exposure/experience/expectations/practice.

Information Needed:

Is the child monolingual? If not, are they a sequential or simultaneous bilingual (multilingual)?

System, or pattern, of language exposure within the home (e.g., mom only speaks _____ to child and dad only speaks _____ to child)?

Are there other English Language Learners in the home? If yes, describe their stage(s) of language acquisition.

Are children normally part of the conversation in home with adults? Is the cultural norm to take turns when speaking? Are children allowed to speak to strangers? Are girls allowed to speak to men?

How does this child compare with others who have faced a similar experience?

Examples:

More Intervention: A child who has multiple older siblings who are learning English as sequential bilinguals and who have multiple errors in their spoken English or analysis using the LE^{3}AP model showing strong learning as a result of exposure, experience, expectation and practice.

Neutral: A child who does not speak any English or so little English that we cannot make judgments based upon this information.

Referral: A child who is a simultaneous bilingual whose older siblings have developed age appropriate English skills, yet this child is still struggling in both English and their native language.

Or place the mark somewhere in-between based upon your data and discussions.

The Why:

We are looking for evidence that either indicates to us that the child has struggles that are expected, given their exposure/experience/expectations/practice, and we need to provide intervention ideas to the family. Or, we are looking for evidence that the child is struggling to learn a skill, and the struggle could be indicative of needing further exploration (a special education referral).

Child's primary language and/or need to learn English (7):

Purpose:

The purpose of this is to understand the experience that the child has in their environment (your city/school district). This is about how the environment as a whole impacts their exposure and experience and their need for English or if the characteristics of the native language are known to impact English language development in the manner in which the student is struggling.

Information Needed:

This item is in part about the nature of the setting (district) and how that relates to rate of learning.

What is the frequency of the language in your district?

What are the characteristics of the language (e.g., are the sounds the same as English sounds or is the prosody the same as English prosody)?

How do the parents describe the "need" to know each of the languages?

How many hours per day does the child need English?

Does the child have a good reason (need) for what you are expecting?

Examples:

More Intervention: A child who lives in an area in which most or all of the needs of the child and family can be achieved without anyone ever speaking English or a child whose primary language has characteristics that commonly cause predictable struggles when transitioning to learning/speaking English.

More Intervention: A child whose parents speak different languages within the home setting, but are inconsistent with regards to what they expect from the child and the exposure they provide to the child.

Neutral: A child who has no exposure to other languages and we have no ability to measure or compare their rate of learning (or not) against peers and other children with similar exposure/experience/expectations/practice.

Referral: A child who speaks a language that is uncommon in your area and they and their family have a significant need for English, yet the child is not learning at a rate similar to other children with the same challenges, even with reasonable exposure and experience.

Referral: A child with a high need to learn English, their parents are learning quickly, their siblings are learning quickly, and the child is struggling (especially if the parents indicate that the same errors are occurring in the native language).

Or place the mark somewhere in-between based upon your data and discussions.

The Why:

This helps the team to understand the impact of the environment on the family, relatives, and friends, which in turn will impact the child. The children who come from languages that are very well supported in the community, especially Spanish, can have a more difficult time transitioning to English (there is research* to document this for Spanish to English). The children who speak a language that is rather uncommon will be in a home environment in which English will be very important, therefore it is much easier to compare their learning with other children and siblings regarding rate of acquisition of English (of course, looking at their personal experience). We are trying to gather data that helps us understand the child as a learner. A child with very little need to learn English (or none) and no evidence of learning English, does not provide us much information to understand if we need more interventions or to make a special education referral. However, a child who has a high personal need, given their personal experiences in their environment, and is not learning like the others in their environment is indicative of a child with a possible/potential disability.

Item 7 is a combination of two previous items, so the examples and "why" were included for both to provide additional information.

*This has nothing to do with the characteristics of the Spanish language or the people who speak Spanish, and everything to do with the need to learn English or not.

Observation (8):

Purpose:

The purpose of this item is to see the concern if at all possible and to try to understand whether or not the concern appears to be adult or setting specific.

Information Needed:

Did the child participate or did they appear too stressed or shy to perform normally?

What were the problem behaviors or issues or skills deficits noted during the observation (if any)? Describe.

Does the child demonstrate different behaviors/skills depending upon environment or adult? Describe.

Examples:

More Intervention: A child who did not demonstrate the behavior of concern in the new setting or a child who listens/interacts normally with non-relative adults and children or a student who demonstrated success with the behavior/skill of concern.

Neutral: A child who appeared overwhelmed by the environment in a way that is normally associated with shyness or normal fear/apprehension of new adults (strangers).

Referral: A child who demonstrated the behaviors of concern during the observation (or skills deficits) and these behaviors of concern (or skills deficits) are outside of the developmental norms for a child this age. Or, children who demonstrate behaviors that are unexpected for what is occurring within the observation environment (e.g., strong emotional reactions to another student entering "their space."). Or a child who tried a skill well within developmental norms and repeatedly demonstrated little or no success.

Or place the mark somewhere in-between based upon your data and discussions.

The Why:

We need to understand what the behavior/skill looks like and when it occurs, and with whom. A child who can behave appropriately in a new environment with strangers is usually not a child with a disability in these areas. Also, a child who can demonstrate skills (or related skills) within the norm for development during observation is usually not a child with a disability. Furthermore, a child who does not behave appropriately for their parents; however, does behave appropriately for school staff, is usually not a child with a disability in these areas. In contrast, if we observe a behavior outside the developmental norms or a lack of a skill that is developmentally appropriate/expected, this could be evidence to support a special education referral. Additionally, a student who demonstrates behaviors that do not coincide with what is occurring in the environment are students of concern (e.g., trying to bite, scratch, spit on, hit another student solely for entering "their" area).

The parent interview (9 A):

Purpose:

The purpose of this item is to gather information related to health, injuries, or illnesses of the child and the learning history within the family.

Information Needed:

Family history for learning?

Child's medical history --- Anything significant (injuries or illnesses)?

Any history of trauma?

Did the child have any history of a lack of opportunity, exposure, other?

Examples:

More Intervention: A child in which there is a family history of success with learning and this child has not had any illnesses or injuries that could potentially be related to a disability.

Neutral: The information that we gained has parts that are indicative of problems, but it is not clear enough to put either above or below neutral. It just does not help us in the decision-making process.

Referral: A child who had a significant injury that could be related to the noted concern (e.g., a head injury and loss of consciousness) and received a medical diagnosis. A child with an illness that is commonly linked to problems with development and learning. A child whose family has a long history of learning problems (and there is not a clear link to a lack of exposure/experience/expectations/practice for the family members).

Or place the mark somewhere in-between based upon your data and discussions.

The Why:

We are looking for evidence that either does not provide indicators that are related to possible disabilities or evidence that is often directly linked to the possibility of a disability. If the child has a medical condition that frequently causes cognitive delays, then it is very possible that the lack of English is not a determining factor and a special education referral is the appropriate action.

Developmental History (9 B):

Purpose:

The purpose of this item is to best understand the developmental milestones achievement of this child, especially in comparison to their family, siblings, peers in their community/culture.

Information Needed:

Are developmental milestones met? If not, describe.

Developmental history compared to siblings, relatives, neighbor children. Take caution to best understand the cultural norms within this child's family, culture, language, and community (think "different," not "better" or "worse").

Examples:

More Intervention: A child who has met all of their developmental milestones at the appropriate times.

Neutral: This can be a child who has not met some developmental milestones, but there are questions the team has regarding their exposure/experience/expectations/practice needed to meet the milestones.

Referral: A child who has been delayed with regards to many of their developmental milestones, and this is uncommon within their family, and there is no evidence to indicate a "logical" reason for the delays that would clearly not be related to a potential disability.

Or place the mark somewhere in-between based upon your data and discussions.

The Why:

This information provides us indicators regarding how the child is developing in comparison to other children. This item is meant to examine development of the child on the milestones that are often measured. Make sure that the milestones that you are using work within the culture of the child (e.g., some cultures do not use forks, spoons, nor knives, so a child that cannot use them in that culture would not provide the team meaningful data).

Examples and Additional Descriptive Information for Selected Items

Examples for Items 1-4:

Item 1:

The child has only been exposed to close family members, all older than them, and he/she is struggling to interact with same age peers--- Mark toward Intervention

The child has had limited exposure to same aged peers and demonstrates some difficulties interacting with same age peers--- Mark toward Neutral

The child has been in multiple daycare settings, each time having to leave due to behavior(s) and the parents are concerned about the same behaviors toward siblings---Mark toward Referral

Item 2:

Child lives in a household in which parents make threats about behavior, but the child is not required to demonstrate that behavior. The children in that household follow very few rules--- Mark toward more intervention (Exposed to correct behavior, yet doesn't experience it much because he/she doesn't need to)

Child lives in a household in which the parents are trying to have the children follow specific expectations and the children are trying to follow those expectations, but consistency is not great--- Mark toward neutral

Child lives in a household in which the parents have set expectations and the children follow those expectations, except this child (who has 2 other siblings in your school who don't demonstrate the behavioral struggles) --- Mark toward referral

Observe for passive resistance versus active resistance for item 2.

Item 3:

Child (3-4 years old) is not producing many intelligle words. The parents respond to the grunts and do not work toward word production--- Mark toward more Intervention

Parents are encouraging the child to approximate words, but often give in and overfunction for the child--- Mark between More Interventions and Neutral*

The parents are practicing words with the child, requiring the child to try the words, but there is no noticeable improvement--- Mark toward Referral

***Maybe up one, maybe down one, depending upon what it reinforces (tantrums or learning).**

Item 3 focuses on expectations of adults (which the adult actions define, not the adult statements.

Item 4:

Child (3-4 years old) is not producing many intelligle words. The parents respond to the grunts and do not work toward word production--- Mark toward more Intervention

Parents are encouraging the child to approximate words, but often give in and overfunction for the child--- Mark between More Interventions and Neutral*

The parents are practicing words with the child, requiring the child to try the words, but there is no noticeable improvement--- Mark toward Referral

***Maybe up one, maybe down one, depending upon what it reinforces (tantrums or learning)**

Focus on the quality, consistency, design, and implementation of the practice/intervention.

Further discussion:

Expectations in the household/daycare (3)

It is critical to understand how the adults and older siblings interact with the child in the daily environment. For example, a child who is not effectively communicating verbally, do adults or siblings guess their "wants" without expecting clear communication? For <u>Motor</u>, is the child allowed to complete activities that require the development of motor skills. For example, what types of foods do they eat and with what utensils? For <u>Adaptive</u>, check to see whether or not the child has had the opportunities and expectations needed to develop in the noted area (e.g., if they cannot drink out of a cup, have they been expected to and for how long?). For <u>Behavior</u>, has the child had a consistent message? Does the message match the expectations of the team (e.g., has the child ever been expected to sit and listen?). **"Lower"*** or different expectations are indicative of a need for more intervention and **"higher"*** expectations without success is more indicative of a referral.

*We need to be careful not to judge in such a way that our biases and value judgements regarding what skills are more or less valuable impact our interpretations. We need to make sure that what we are judging the level of skill demonstrated, not a perceived value of the skill.

Intervention (Practice) description (4)

The team needs to determine well in advance of talking about special education (unless there is a clear medical condition impacting the child or there is a high likelihood of an intellectual disability) what exactly is the concern. That is, don't just look at the area(s) of concern, but also look at the environment, expectations, and what (if anything) has been done to address the concern. For <u>Behavior</u>, has the child had a consistent message? Does the message match the expectations of the team (e.g., has the child ever been expected to sit and listen?). For <u>Adaptive</u>, check to see whether or not the child has had the opportunities and expectations to develop in the noted area (e.g., if they cannot drink out of a cup, have they been expected to and, if yes, for how long). If they cannot zip their coat, have they been expected to (and for how long)? For <u>Communication</u>, what has their environment been like (i.e., has it been a language rich environment or not, and in what languages?). If not, how can you measure the skill? The main difference between factor 3 and 4 is: **Was anything systematic ever done to address the concern? If yes, what were the results?** As with many of these items, is the behavior or skill developmentally appropriate within the culture of the student? How do you know? And, if the student was "taught" a new skill did they actually know what skill they were supposed to be learning? How do you know?

So, place a mark on the chart based upon the likely impact. If the interventions haven't been targeted to a specific need then the mark goes more toward the need for more interventions. If the interventions have been targeted and the results are poor compared to like peers, then the mark goes more toward Referral.

Parental literacy in "primary" language (5)

This can impact the child's vocabulary and language structures. At the younger ages, the issue is more about vocabulary than language structure, and the vocabulary issues go from minor impact to greater impact as the child ages from 3 to 5 years of age. Limited vocabulary slows the rate of learning and makes some content much more difficult to access. Please note, when combined with poverty, the impact on vocabulary **can** be extreme. So, place a mark on the chart based upon the likely impact. If the parent has limited literacy in the language shared with their child place a mark in the range of more intervention needed. If the parent is literate in the language shared with their child (and the concern is language development based) place a mark in the possible referral range. Base this on facts and not appearances.

This is a great place to give an example regarding whether or not our tests really work. Imagine you don't know about the home environment of the two students you recently tested for expressive and receptive language. Imagine that the two students both received a standard score of 85. One of the two students is in a home in which the parents left school during the third grade and who do not read in the shared language. The other student is in a home in which both parents have a college education and both are strong readers.

Reading is highly correlated to vocabulary. However, there is no agreement on "size of vocabulary." Which of the following words should be counted: light, lighter, lightest? Are we counting active vocabulary, passive vocabulary, or both? And, how do we count/measure 20,000 to 30,000 words? For this discussion, we will use a common number within that field of study that indicates a non-reader has an active vocabulary of around 2,500 words and someone with post high school education has an active vocabulary of 10,000-20,000 words.

So, the first child was in an environment in which they mastered every word they were exposed to, yet wasn't exposed to a great deal of the vocabulary within the tests we used. The second child was exposed to all of the vocabulary needed to score well above average on the test, yet scored at the bottom of the average. Without knowing about and considering the environment of the students, we cannot accurately interpret the results of our tests.

Approach taken with regards to English Learning (6)

Has the child received direct instruction, indirect instruction (siblings are learning English), or no instruction? What was the intensity of the instruction? In relationship to the exposure and instruction, how much progress has the child made? If multiple languages are spoken at home, what are the percentages, is it systematic (e.g., mom only speaks _____ to the child and dad only speaks _____)? You need a team member who is familiar with and understands the impact(s) of simultaneous versus sequential bilingual if the child is already learning English. As a team, discuss this information and determine whether it, as a whole, is indicative of needing an intervention to address the issues or indicative of needing to make a referral for special education. Then place the mark in the matrix that represents the discussion.

Child's primary language and/or need to learn English (7)

Take into consideration your community, and the native language of the child and also characteristics of the native language versus English. If you are evaluating a 3-4-year-old with little or no exposure to English, this is less critical or not critical (which means your team should mark neutral in the matrix). Does the child have notable exposure to English (older siblings all trying to learn and practice English) and/or a language notably different from English (e.g., Vietnamese does not blend letter sounds like English), then this needs to be considered. Also, if your community has a large population speaking the language in question or a very small population, this can impact the child's development. The best predictor of learning a new language for children is the need to learn the language. Does the child speak a language that is common in the environment, and therefore only needs English for school? Does the child speak a language that is uncommon, and the parents need the help of the child for navigating the environment? Discuss these possibilities or issues and try to understand the need of the child to learn English (the more that is competing with this need, the more likely more intervention is the correct response). Lower need(s) to learn English are more indicative of interventions. Higher need(s) to learn English, with success levels below expectation as related to exposure/opportunity, are more indicative of a special education referral. There is additional discussion on this topic throughout the book.

Observation (8)

For all children who do not have clear and significant impairments caused by clear medical issues and/or moderate to severe intellectual disabilities, an observation is needed in an environment that allows the child opportunities to play and interact. It is critical that it is a comfortable environment for the child. When this is not possible, staff needs to understand the normal reaction(s) of children this age to new environments and new adults (i.e., if the child appears apprehensive or fearful it could be developmentally appropriate, and the observation then would be of limited value). Then discuss as a team and place the appropriate mark into the matrix. For example, if the child behaves for some adults and not others, it is likely more intervention(s) is the appropriate choice. **Is the concern adult or setting specific? Are you observing a skills deficit or a performance deficit? How do you know?**

The parent interview (9 A)

This will tell you the family history of learning, and behavioral norms for the child. Several of these areas have been addressed above. The key is looking for data that would either support that the child is a capable learner (and therefore a special education referral is not supported) or the child profile indicates issues/problems outside the normal range (and therefore a special education referral is supported).

Appendix C (second half for Preschool Version) provides information regarding using the data to design interventions or support either a special education referral or special education evaluation.

Chapter 6: Data Analysis

Do You Know Your School and District Data?

The data regarding proportional or disproportional distribution within special education is something that should be known prior to starting the matrix process. For example, if you did not know that only 60% of the students in your school, or your district, are successful with the core instruction, you would not know that the student you are examining could be a casualty of a system that is not working for students in general. If you did not know that your district is qualifying Black/African American students as intellectually disabled at twice the rate of the state, you would not know to go the extra mile when evaluating a student who is Black/African American to ensure accuracy. If you did not know that your district uses the category of Specific Learning Disability for all students in special education at a rate of 37%, but uses it at 70% for the ELL/Special Education Dually qualified students, you would not know there was a problem in that area. If you did not know that 100% of your dually qualified students all speak the same language, and you have 22 languages in your district, you would not know there is a problem. Examining your data helps to ensure that you are not part of creating or maintaining the problem, instead you have the opportunity to be part of solving the problem. These are real life examples and not even the more extreme examples.

In order for a school to be able to say a student is not making reasonable progress, they need to know (not think) that their system is working for the vast majority of students and that their work is leading to proportional results. In order to do this, the school (and hopefully the district) needs to analyze their own data.

As a first step, you will need to answer this first set of questions, which are more global in nature. Later we will provide a list of additional questions that require more specific data to help provide answers. Researching the answers to these questions will lead to the systems level and building level analysis needed to understand the nature and location of the problems.

- How do you know that your students as a group are making progress? In order to answer this, you should know the growth rates of your students on the local and state tests as compared to other students in schools in your district, around your state and in the research.

- If you cannot prove average to above-average rates of growth (from the answer to the question above), how do you know the student in question is not actually a curriculum or instruction causality?

- What are the graduation rates of cohorts of students in your district that attended your school, and how do they compare to other groups? All students? ELL students? Special Education students? Dually qualified students?

- What are the demographics of the students who are referred for special education evaluations, who are evaluated, and who are qualified for special education services in your school and district? For example, if 20% of your students receive F/R lunch, do only 20% of your special education students receive F/R lunch? Or, your district has 13% of the students qualified for special education services, but within your ELL student population 28% of the students are qualified for special education.

Once you know the patterns for your school and your district and you have compared them to state and national data, introspection is crucial. If your building (and district) has clear issues with over qualification by race, language learner status, ethnicity, etcetera, how will you be able to factor that into your decision-making process?

Please note, most schools and districts currently have problems in these areas, so it is crucial that staff do not lose hope or become overly critical once these problems are identified. Blame and/or shame do not work in the problem-solving process, and actually lead to slow results or no positive results. Instead, staff need to have real and open discussions on why these results are the way they are currently. In education, it is profoundly rare to find a staff member who is not a caring and loving individual (even if they try to play it otherwise). We are good people doing hard work. So, take these crucial and difficult conversations seriously, yet focus on solutions and not blame. Once a path toward achieving better results has been set forth, it will take 3-5 years to see large, measurable change.

The following pages contain questions that can lead to further understanding of where the problems are within your school and district. The list of questions cannot cover all the possibilities, especially knowing that new questions can and will arise as data reveals problems. This list provides a starting point, and it is far more extensive than Steve has seen in use in any of the 200+ districts that he has worked with in Washington and other states on data dives and analysis. The good news is that districts are starting to conduct in-depth data analysis (and, luckily, it really is not all that hard).

How to Analyze School and District Data to Help Make Better Decisions

The short answer: easy, get all of the data and start asking and answering questions. The long answer is to start on the surface and keep digging deeper, asking more questions, as the following steps are going to delve into. The following questions are meant to be examples and are not all encompassing. Hopefully this will get teams off to a good start and then their individual circumstances will lead them to ask other questions.

1) What percentage of your district population is qualified for special education services?
2) What percentage of your district is qualified for ELL services?

3) What percentage of your special education qualified students are also ELL qualified students?

4) What percentage of ELLs are qualified for special education services?

5) Make a graph that shows the data for elementary schools from question number 4 by individual school.

6) How do the results of questions above look? That is, is there proportionality or not?

7) What percentage of your district is qualified for F/R meals?

8) What percentage of your special education qualified students are also qualified for F/R meals?

9) What percentage of you students qualified for F/R meals are qualified for special education?

10) How do the results of these recent questions look? That is, is there proportionality or not?

11) Break down the results from above by building. Is there any correlation to ELL eligibility and/or F/R lunch percentages by building?

12) How does that compare to the state average? Your first goal is to at least be on the positive side of the state averages, knowing that the state averages might also be demonstrating systems level problems.

The next level of depth:

13) What is the percentage by language spoken for each of the language groups within your district? Are there any tendencies by building?

14) What are the percentages, by language, for your dually qualified students? Do this overall and by disability.

15) For all students qualified for special education, what is the percentage in each of the disability categories?

16) What is the percentage by language group (major groups for this item) represented within your special education qualified group by disability category?

17) Create a column in the spreadsheet for each of the following for each disability category listed by percentage: all students (with ELL included), all students (without ELL included), all ELL students, all ELL students (just major language groups), ELL students from rare language groups. This item is more powerful in medium to large size districts.

18) Do the numbers appear logical or not? The percentages/proportions should be roughly equal (e.g., 17% of all students are language learners and 17% of the students qualified for special education are language learners, or anywhere between 16-18%).

19) How do your district's numbers compare to state and national numbers (found on the state report cards and the OSEP website, respectively)? Sometimes a request must be made, but this is public information.

Given that there will be year-to-year variations, and results may be better or worse, trend lines must be positively related to the end goal. If there are significant differences, teams need to get together and have real conversations regarding why the differences exist and what the possible solutions are for the disproportionalities. No race, ethnic, nor language group has inherently higher rates of disabilities (qualification rates do not equal disability rates).

20) Does the distribution make sense based upon data? Within a building: Be careful with small data sets.

21) Do the categories of qualification match the percentages at the district level? In other words, if SLD is used 37% of the time across the district, is each building using SLD 37% of the time with their dually qualified students? Is there variation by other groups?

22) Within each building, are there specific problems related to any of the disability categories?

23) Within each building, are there specific problems related to any of the linguistic groups?

24) Within the school psychologists and speech and language pathologists, are there staff members who are qualifying students in larger or smaller numbers?

The first time this is done, **for any major "problem area,"** an individual will need to examine the specific students (likely needing to examine the actual files) and answer the following:

25) What percentage of the students within that group were qualified within the district?

26) Of the students qualified within the district, which buildings were those students qualified in?

27) What was the date of the qualification for ELL students qualified for SLD or SLI? Using this information, what each student's language acquisition level at that time? Create a chart for this.

It is common that many of the students were qualified for SLD (often SLI, too) while they were at language acquisition level 1 and 2, and there is no data to support the problem existed (or exists) in their native language. This conflicts directly with the regulation that "limited English proficiency" is a factor that must be ruled out.

Chapter 7: Belief Systems

Our Personal Journey

We are all experiencing our own personal journey, and everyone's journey is unique. Learning how to determine whether or not a student needs more interventions, or if a special education referral is more appropriate, is a long learning journey, and one that Steve is still traveling. This journey is made easier or more difficult depending upon each person's willingness and ability to reflect upon their acculturation, their beliefs, their actions (practices) and their results.

We are acculturated from the day we start to understand what is occurring around us. Acculturation is combined with knowledge and this creates belief systems that eventually leads to actions and practices at work. Our practices lead to results, good, bad, or other. We know our results with regards to disproportionality are poor. Our results are not poor because we are actively and knowingly doing bad things (actions or practices), given educators are good and caring people. In order for us to achieve different results, we need to understand what is occurring with our belief systems and acculturation, and how these impact our practices. Then, we can modify our practices and achieve different results. Key questions each person needs to ask themselves, whatever the problem might be, are: "Am I part of creating or maintaining this problem? Or am I part of solving the problem? Our results on disproportionality are very poor, what is my role? Can I possibly know the answer if I don't know the data for my school, district, and state?" Highly unlikely!

One principal that Steve worked with told him, "all of my best teachers are worried about not doing enough and not doing a good enough job and all of my weakest teachers believe they have nothing to learn and are working harder than everyone else." We (the authors) believe that when there is a situation at work (or in life) in which things do not go right or do not go well, the very first thoughts should be about the following: What could I have done differently? What could I have done better? What can I learn from this? This mindset is likely to lead to learning from our mistakes and remaining a learner throughout our career (and life for that matter).

Therefore, each of us needs to examine our belief systems and our acculturation, so we understand if we are helping to create some of the disproportionality or if we are part of maintaining existing disproportionality. This process is difficult and at times painful. However, it is necessary for us to figure out how we can be part of the solution, a goal each and every one of us should strive to achieve.

The following pages are meant to provoke thinking and to provide you with examples to help stimulate your own thinking and the thinking of others. Hopefully this will also evoke emotions, as emotions help us to remember what we have learned. For example: a parent may try to teach their 3-4-year-old a new word that isn't important to the child, and the child just does not learn the new word. But when the parent gets cut off by another driver and responds, "$ *&^ @#$ $#@#," the child, only having heard this phrase once, uses it the following day in correct context, with correct intonation, and with emotion. Don't forget, this will happen in front of your parents, or friends.

So, as you read this, think about:

Acculturation → Belief Systems → Practices → Results

Think about whether you are a part of creating, maintaining, or fixing the problems in your system, and what evidence you have to support your view of where you stand in your system. We are good and caring people, we can use the emotions to fuel a desire to learn more, change our practices, and support others to change their practices.

The reason for this is that our results occur not by chance, but as a result of our practices. Our practices occur based upon what we believe in and our belief systems are a combination of our knowledge and our acculturation. How we are acculturated creates a lens through which we see the world.

The stories in the following pages provide examples of this. We are sharing these with you to build knowledge and to encourage you to continuously monitor and challenge personal beliefs and practices.

Overview

1) **We See What We Are Acculturated To See:** Real world examples of acculturation creating a lens.

2) **Steve's Personal Educator Journey:** Real world example of developing over time, making mistakes, gaining new knowledge, learning, changing practices.

3) **Steve Hirsh's and Walter Gilliam's Research:** Research that shows the impact of our biases.

4) **Monolingual Nation:** Real world examples that help us see what could be unrealistic expectations and/or a lack of reasonable expectations.

5) **Literacy and Intelligence:** Knowledge to help us see things differently.

6) **Poverty:** Research that shows our results, and indicates biases.

7) **Qualification Versus Disability:** Research that shows that our results do not follow logical patterns, nor our "spoken" beliefs.

8) **Reading and Referrals:** Research that indicates our system, results and beliefs have significant flaws.

9) **Impact of Race on Qualification Rates:** Research that shows our results, again, do not follow logical patterns, nor our "spoken" beliefs

10) **Qualification Does Not Equal Disability:** A summary of data and research that show how unlikely it is that qualification rate actually equals disability rate in our system.

Then, the chapter ends with a write-up regarding the "takeaways" for each of these areas.

1. We See What We Are Acculturated to See

The following three examples are meant to help you understand that we see what we are acculturated to see. Our acculturation provides a lens which we look through and that changes our view of the world.

Ushani is one of the few people on earth who is a German/Sri Lankan. Sri Lanka is an island in the Indian Ocean, just south of India. Therefore, it's easy to assume that Germans and Sri Lankans do not commonly meet one another in such a way that relationships are likely to begin. Additionally, of the Germans and Sri Lankans who do meet, not all of them speak a common language. Then, of the Germans and Sri Lankans who do meet and who do speak a common language, not very many are likely to form a romantic relationship, get married, and have children.

People who meet Ushani struggle greatly in figuring out her heritage and make many assumptions. Ushani has had numerous experiences in which someone has spoken Spanish to her, assuming that she is a Latina, only to have Steve respond. This tends to leave the person completely dumbfounded. They probably wonder why the Latina* doesn't speak Spanish, but the older white guy does (some folks have literally told Steve that it is confusing to them to have an older white guy speaking Spanish with them). When Ushani is around people who are Black or African American, she is often thought to be a light skinned Black or African American woman. Then, there are times in which people believe that Ushani is a woman from India (to her Sri Lankan relatives, this is totally illogical). Virtually no one guesses that Ushani is from Sri Lanka. This is in large part because people rarely have a mental picture of what someone from Sri Lanka looks like (a lack of knowledge, a lack of this being part of one's acculturation). Did you have a picture of what someone from Sri Lanka might look like prior to this? Nobody ever guesses German, and many Germans have struggled to "see" Ushani as a German. Some Germans think she is Turkish; others think she is Black. A friend of the family once asked her mother when she considered moving back to Germany, "Don't you think it will be difficult for a Black child to grow up in Germany?"

People are not acculturated to imagine someone who looks like Ushani as German. Acculturation created lenses for each of these groups that impacted their decision making and their actions, like it does for all of us.

*Steve usually uses the terms Latino(a) and Black, instead of Hispanic and African-American, given his acculturation. This is an important point about cultural competence versus cultural responsiveness that we will discuss near the end of this chapter. Do you know any of your habits that were created by your acculturation?

The following example is from Steve's experience as a child with an extreme speech impediment and aphasia illustrates how acculturation and belief systems can create lenses through which people interpret the world. Steve's grandmother told him the following story many times. When Steve was 3 to 4 years old, Steve's parents were convinced by their friends that he must be "retarded," the term of the time. Eventually, his parents took him to Seattle Children's Hospital for an evaluation. The first person who saw Steve was a Speech and Language Pathologist, and this person told Steve's parents that not only was he not "retarded," he might actually be bright. That same afternoon Steve was evaluated by either Nancy or Hal Robinson (The Robinson Center on the University of Washington Campus) and Steve's parents were told he was gifted. A strange day in the life of a child who had no idea what was going on. The jury is still out regarding who was right (that is meant of be funny ☺).

During the time Steve's parents were convinced by others that he might be "retarded," at an age of 3-4 years old, Steve was reading and playing chess with adults. Most folks were sure Steve was just looking at the books and they didn't believe his mother's claim that he was reading (given nobody could understand what he was saying). The chess was pretty hard to deny, since people could see it occur. So, what is the point of this story? As a child Steve could not effectively communicate and was therefore seen by others to be cognitively limited, or "dumb." In our society, people who don't speak English are often seen as unlikely to be intelligent*. However, in our schools with language learners, it is possible that the smartest child in the school does not yet speak English.

*Steve has noticed during his training events that people in the audience who speak English as a second or later language all nod their heads in agreement when this point is made. These folks have confirmed this in discussions during breaks.

Have you ever seen an interview with Tiger Woods in which he talks about how much it bothers him that he is virtually never seen as an Asian man? Do you ever think of Tiger Woods as an Asian man? Or, solely as a Black or African American man? Tiger Woods expresses how he sees this as disrespectful to his mother and the heritage he has inherited from her.

There are many other examples in our world, yet this provides a window into how acculturation creates a lens through which we view our world. We need to examine ourselves to see how our acculturation is creating our lens.

2. Steve's Personal Educator Journey: The Painful Life Lessons

When Steve was in graduate school there was no coursework on the assessment of language learners; it was not even discussed. Steve began his career in the Tacoma School District and he quickly realized that he lacked skills in the area of evaluating language learners. Then he learned that finding information on this topic was next to impossible. This was pre-Google.

The first event to shape Steve's experience was a little boy who walked into his office with a doctor's script that said "ADHD, qualifies for special education as a student with an Other Health Impairment." School psychologists often do not take this any better than medical doctors would take school psychologists making medical diagnosis and sending the families to the doctor's office. Steve called the doctor and asked him how he made the diagnosis, and the doctor responded, "I was educated at Harvard." After hearing this a few times Steve expressed his lack of care regarding the doctor's education. The doctor finally said, "I interviewed the family." Steve responded, "You speak Vietnamese?" The doctor then told Steve to do things that would be anatomically difficult to achieve,

Steve responded, and eventually the doctor hung up the phone (it is likely Steve was having a better time than the doctor). It was later discovered that this student did not have ADHD and the family had no idea what had occurred.

Steve moved on with his career, eventually landing in a district that had a large percentage of Spanish speaking students in special education. Steve decided that he wanted to be bilingual and bi-literate, so he started taking night classes. After a year, he might have achieved the ability to ask where the bathroom is or order a beer, but not much more. With a great deal of luck, Steve ended up eating dinner with Dr. Stephen Krashen, one of the leading experts in the world on language acquisition. Dr. Krashen told Steve what he needed to do, and it was all about comprehensible input. So, Steve started to read books in Spanish, starting with kindergarten level books, until he mastered those, then first grade level books, and when he mastered those, second grade level books (reading The Mouse and the Motorcycle with great excitement), and so on.

Steve eventually had a dilemma. The only books at his level that he could find were the Twilight series, something rather hard on his ego (please note, this story is going somewhere). Steve thought he was safe reading this at school, and was walking to the staff lounge holding this book when a nice little girl that Steve knew well asked him if she could borrow the book after he was done with it. Steve first thought "Why?" believing she could not read the book because she was qualified for special education for reading, had never lived in a Spanish speaking country, and had no formal education in Spanish. Steve told her, "I will buy you brand new copies of the books if you stop by my office each week to, 1) Tell me about what you read, 2) Tell me about what you liked, 3) Tell me about what you think will happen next." This did not go as Steve thought it would go. Not only did she read every one of these books, she provided Steve replies to his questions ad nauseam. The point to this story is that not only was she qualified for special education for reading in English, not only had she never been formally educated in Spanish, not only was she reading at a higher level in Spanish than in English, Steve was the school psychologist who had qualified her for special education. This was a painful learning moment for Steve. A moment that required a lot of reflection. We saw this young lady many years later, and she gave Steve a big hug. She remembered talking about the books and she still has the books.

Soon after this Steve began working for the Kent School District as the ESA Coach (the coach for all of the school psychologists, speech and language pathologists, occupational therapists, and physical therapists). He was offered the opportunity to start the district supported ELL graduate level program through Heritage University. This is where the work on the ELL Critical Data Process began, and the puzzle pieces started coming together.

The point of these stories is that each of us is on a journey of skills development. This can only occur if each of us is honest with ourselves about our mistakes, honest with ourselves regarding the impact of our acculturation, honest with ourselves about our skills (or lack of skills), honest with ourselves about our knowledge (or lack of knowledge) and if we do something to work on our own issues (Yoda said, "There is no try, there is do and not do"). We also need to be willing to examine our own issues around belief systems and race, in order to improve and focus on making a difference in disproportionality.

3. Steve Hirsch's Research

Steve Hirsch is a school psychologist in Washington State who has been a leader within the state school psychologist association for many years. Dr. Hirsch completed the following research as part of other ongoing projects and presented the information at the state school psychologist conference, trying to help people understand that we have biases that we are not aware of, and that those biases are impacting our work. The slides below represent the results after staff were given identical data on four students, in which the only difference was the name of the student and the country of origin.

The first slide shows that, with identical data, the Latino students were significantly more likely to be referred for special education evaluations. The second slide, with identical data for each of the students, shows that there are significantly different rates of recommendation to complete an early re-evaluation for the possibility to exit the student from special education, based solely upon their name and country of origin (based upon the subtle and likely unknown biases of the participants).

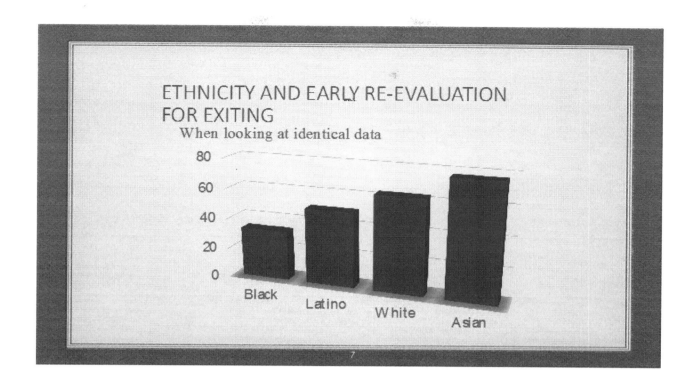

ETHNICITY AND EARLY RE-EVALUATION FOR EXITING
When looking at identical data

We all want to believe that we do not have biases, yet we all have them. It is a natural part of being human. We need to have the courage to examine our biases and the impact of those upon our work.

Another excellent example of research on biases is the research completed at Yale University by lead researcher Walter Gilliam. This research had a group of teachers watching videos of children playing, and they were asked to identify the challenging behaviors as they saw them occur in the videos. There were four children, one White boy, one White girl, one Black boy, and one Black girl. The researchers used eye scanning technology to watch the eyes of the teachers. The teachers watched the Black boys significantly more than the other children. The interesting part is that there was no challenging behavior at all occurring in the videos. The research has other very important components and is well worth reading (if you Google Walter Gilliam and research on biases, you will find this and other research articles). As noted earlier in this book, Black boys are identified as behaviorally disabled at a much higher rate than other children. What if that is a result of school staff expecting them to behave poorly, watching them more closely than other children, and reacting differently given those expectations? Is it also possible that these children behave differently because they feel that they are being treated unfairly, singled out?

What if the difference between proportional and disproportional is more about us, the educators, than it is about the students?

4. Monolingual Nation: Our Expectations of Our Students

Are we really the "monolingual" nation???

Are our expectations of our students based upon a knowledge of the challenges that they face? And, do we have any personal experience related to the depth of those challenges? We have created the following food for thought. However, a small joke before beginning: What do you call someone who speaks 3 or more languages? Multilingual. What do you call someone who speaks 2 languages? Bilingual. What do you call someone who speaks just one language? American.... ☺

Steve was studying in Valencia, Spain, in a large language school. There were over 100 students, mostly from Northern Europe. There were only 2 Americans, and both Americans were receiving a LARGE quantity of negativity regarding Americans and Americans' ethnocentricity. "You people don't even care enough to learn another language." After about a week of this, Steve responded (in a nice way) that he had had enough. Eventually after more commentary, Steve pointed out that they used their best English speakers/writers to create signs in English and every single one of the signs had an error. They originally thought this was impossible. Steve, at their urging, took them around the building to every sign with English text and explained the errors (all the signs had errors). This eventually became a game, with all the students who were attempting to learn English taking Steve around the campus to talk about every sign they could find.

During an experience in a different language school in Spain, Steve had three teachers who all had significant exposure to English. Two had their master's degrees in teaching English and one had been teaching English in the Spanish public school system for decades (one subject area within the day). One evening, we went to dinner together with the condition that dinner was going to occur in English. One person gave up immediately, another could form sentences in English with a great deal of effort (about the time the conversation moved on the next topic), and the third person could hold a conversation in English on basic daily activity topics. Functioning in your non-dominant language truly is difficult.

In Sri Lanka, in the big city of Colombo, it is not difficult to find someone who speaks English (it is very common throughout the schools to teach English). During one of their trips Steve and Ushani stayed in a hotel outside of Colombo. The hotel stated that it would always have someone available who spoke English. One day Steve and Ushani needed some towels, and went to the front desk. The front desk sent for the person who could speak English. Steve and Ushani then worked with this person for quite some time trying to express what they needed (this could have been a Saturday Night Live skit, or a Candid Camera scene).

After visiting Sri Lanka, Steve and Ushani visited Ushani's family in Germany. After a few days, Steve told Ushani she didn't need to interpret any longer for him, he was content to just smile and nod his head. Have you ever noticed a language learner looking at you, smiling and nodding their head? Have you ever done this with your spouse, significant other, or a good friend when you didn't understand the topic that they kept talking about? Do you know what that means? It means they (or you) got tired of concentrating and trying to make sense of what the others were saying and chose to just nod and smile.

The point to this story is not to pick on any other group, but to challenge the idea that everyone else speaks multiple languages, that everyone speaks English, that speaking a little bit of another language is being bilingual or multilingual. The point is that we are not just expecting our English Language Learners to know something about their store or business, we are not expecting them to hold simple conversations. Instead, we are expecting them to function on high stakes tests. And, if they do not function well on these tests we wonder whether or not they have a disability....

Camino de Santiago

This sign in Spanish and English is an example of the type of sign seen in Spain. It is highly unlikely that anyone who speaks only English would understand what they are facing along this path. The English should say:

Attention Cyclists

Steep Hills in/for 15 kilometers

Ride with caution.

Without actually being on the path it is impossible to know if the sign is meant to say "in" 15 kilometers or "for" 15 kilometers. Spanish speakers and readers, why would they have a sign that warns bicyclists about a something that is an hour away (if you believe it means "in" 15 kilometers)?

How many of you studied Spanish in high school and/or college? Some of you for years, right? Why couldn't you understand what the sign said? Because, it is hard to reach a functional level in a second or higher language. Do you expect your English Language Learners to function at this level or higher? If they don't, do they get referred for a possible special education evaluation? How many years are they given and what levels of support, prior to a judgment that their progress just is not good enough...?

5. Literacy and Intelligence

A belief held here in the United States is that people who cannot read are on average of lower intelligence. There could be some correlation in countries with exceptionally high rates of literacy. However, some knowledge is needed to reduce the overgeneralization of this belief. There are roughly 7,000 languages on earth and about 100 years ago only an estimated 2,000 of these languages had a written system. Some of the remaining 5,000 languages had written forms, but only very few people knew them. Over the last 100 years, people from these 5,000 or so languages have in many cases worked very hard to create a written form for their language (or a standardized and agreed upon form of their language), fearing that the language would be "lost" if it did not have a known, documented and used written form. Some of these languages have only had a written form for roughly 50 years.

The Kent School District is in King County (along with Seattle). Within King County there is a very large Somali population. What we have read about the Somali language indicates that there were 5-6 written forms for Somali that were not widely known or widely used. Then, in the late 1960's a new written form was agreed upon. Given how young this written form is, the literacy rate in Somali is currently estimated at under 30%. There are many languages that are in this same place right now. Therefore, in situations like this, a lack of reading skill is more likely related to a lack of exposure, experience, expectation and practice. And, in situations like this, a lack of reading skills is not likely to be related to intelligence.

6. Poverty

When working with large groups of educators and asking the following question, rarely is there someone who is willing to raise their hand and say "yes":

Do people in poverty have higher rates of disabilities?

The answer is yes, but not based upon what some people might be thinking. The answer is yes because people with disabilities have higher rates of poverty. Reading deficits are extremely common within people with disabilities, given the most common disabilities center around learning disabilities and some other disabilities have reading deficits as a common factor. In our country, someone who cannot read, on average, is going to have a much more difficult time obtaining a living wage job. Therefore, there is some causation from disability to poverty, and a small correlation of poverty to higher rates of disability. Sadly, though, the research shows that students in poverty are frequently over identified for special education even though the correlations/causations noted above are about their parents and not about our students. And, poverty does not cause disabilities, but instead can be linked to less exposure and experience, and sometimes less time for parent support. These factors do not make a student disabled, but instead create a situation in which a student is likely to have a more difficult time in school. The following pages document the research Steve completed in Washington State, showing that our qualification rates and our poverty rates are linked, sadly.

7. Qualification vs. Disability

Special Education Qualification Rates in Washington State and the Link to Free and Reduced Lunch Rates

Steve examined the data for 295 school districts. No district was purposely left out of the data, with the exception of school districts in the data set that were(are) not actually comprehensive school districts (e.g., School for the Blind). Therefore, with a set of 250 districts, it is highly unlikely that any district missed would have impacted the noted trends.

For 16 districts the special education eligibility percentages fell below 10% of the total student population. For 15 of these 16 school districts, the average student population in the districts was 145 students (145 is the average of the total student population and not just the total for the special education population; the 16th was a medium sized district noted separately below).

There were 32 districts with special education eligibility percentages above 18% of the total student population. The average student population across these districts was 392 students. As above, 392 represents the total student population and not just the special education population. The highest percentage of children qualified as children with disabilities was 37.5% of the district. Can there really be a district where 37.5% of the children have disabilities? That district happened to have a population in which 75% of the students were of Native American heritage. Did those two numbers happen together totally by chance? That is very unlikely and the results are inappropriate.

In the State of Washington, 45.9% of the students were on Free or Reduced Lunch (at the time of this research). The average percentage of F/R Lunch for the districts below 10% special education qualification rate was 24%. The average percentage of F/R Lunch for the districts above 18% was 75.6%.

The only medium/large district with a percentage below 10% of the student population qualified for special education services was the Issaquah School District, at 8.8%. It is interesting to note that Issaquah School District has some of the highest state test scores noted during this research.

Although the F/R Lunch difference is extreme, there is no way to prove that it is a causal factor. Yet, many research studies have indicated that poverty is a very high predictor of special education qualification. This occurs even though it would be very hard to argue, beyond a minimal percentage difference, that poverty has any correlation to rates of disabilities, and no causal relationship either. It is important to note that the causal or correlational issues we are talking about are the parents of our children, not our children. Therefore, the correlation becomes even weaker when looking at the children. That is, the small correlation of the parent in poverty to disability of the parent would be multiplied by the small correlation of parent to child disability (inheritance) to achieve an extremely small correlational value/predictive value.

It is interesting to note that virtually all of the districts on the extremes of the range have very small student populations. In all of these cases, one or only a few people are leading the qualification decisions.

It would be hard to examine this data and not see the human impact on the work. We have a lot of power in influencing outcomes, and, hopefully, a lot to think about in our daily work to bring about positive student outcomes.

You will see these points repeated throughout the book because we have a very hard time seeing ourselves involved in any of the negative results ("we" being that universal we). However, most staff have not examined the data for their schools and district. We need to have the courage to look closely at our work and to begin to solve problems as they appear. The data is not the way it is because so few people are involved in the problem. Wherever there is a problem, a lot of staff members were involved in creating or maintaining the problem (remember, not bad people, just bad results). This could seem to contradict what was said above. However, in the problem noted above just a few people had "control" over the outcome, yet many people had input and involvement. So, the big "we" could have stopped the problem if they had seen it as a problem. We need as many people as possible involved in the solutions. If you know the data and/or have a strong basis in working on belief systems, you can be an active and planned part of the solution. The goal is to be an active part of the solution instead of just hoping your work will be part of the solution.

The following quote from the University of Texas at Austin is included to provide additional insight into this issue.

Education and Transition to Adulthood, Information on Learning Disabilities, available at: http://www.utexas.edu/cola/etag/Related%20Sites/Learning-Disabilities.php

> Although the research focus has primarily been on the disproportionate labeling of racial minorities with LD, the research team found that differences in the rates of being labeled are more dramatic by socioeconomic status (SES) than by race. The odds of being labeled with LD are much higher among low SES than high SES high school students, regardless of whether the student is Black or white. In fact, low SES white high school students are as likely as low SES Black or Hispanic high school students to be labeled with LD, but much greater proportions of racial minorities are in that high-risk low SES group.

In contrast to Black and white high school students, high SES Hispanic high school students are as likely as low SES Hispanic high school students to be labeled with LD. <u>The team found that disproportionate labeling of Hispanic students with learning disabilities in high school is attributable to the over-labeling of language minorities.</u>

The team also found that students attending higher poverty schools are actually less likely to be labeled with LD, and that systematic differences in academic achievement by SES, race, and linguistic status are a major factor in disproportionality.

Underline added for emphasis.

8. Reading and Referrals

Qualification rates are not equivalent to disability rates

Specific Learning Disability is a category that was, more or less, created for the special education world. It is the only category that greatly increased beyond population change from 1975 to 2004, when the special education population in the United States peaked between 2000 and 2004 and has since been dropping. It is the main category to decrease in size since 2004. The SLD category tripled in numbers from 1975 to 2004, eventually being the category in which roughly 50% of all special education students were qualified. Interestingly enough, the decrease in this category started with the federal law that included the usage of RTI qualification. It is easy to see the decrease in the SLD category aligning with the increased usage of RTI within the school systems. Although it should be simple to state the exact percentage of the students qualified in this category, it just isn't. As of the day that I typed this sentence in 2020, I found one website (official government sites) stating 33.6% and another stating 38.8%. It is safe to state, also using the data I have seen from hundreds of districts, that the percentage is in the mid-thirties. Always check multiple sources. Within my own state they had ELL statistics that were completely different because they were calculating two different things but using the same label.

The following quotes provide a lot to think about and are followed by ways to mitigate these concerns.

Dr. Carnine (University of Oregon) testifying to the Senate
  ▸ "Moving to a response to intervention model can dramatically reduce the long-term failure that is often associated with the IQ-achievement discrepancy formula. 70 to 90 percent of

the most at risk children in Kindergarten through 2nd grade can be brought to the average range with effective instruction."

The research into well-implemented RTI or Tiered Intervention has shown that many students who would have previously qualified under SLD have been appropriately served (and have better long-term outcomes) through interventions implemented within the general education setting.

Dr. Torgesen from Florida

- "Within 1 year following the intervention, 40% of the children were found to be no longer in need of special education services."
- This was only 8 weeks of intervention at 2 hours per day and the children were labeled "with severe reading disabilities..."

Whether looking at this research or the research on the Lindamood Bell approach, it is easy to see that short-term intensive intervention that is focused on the specific needs of the children shows us that many children do not have disabilities, but instead are casualties of our system. The research noted above was with children considered to have "severe reading disabilities." Studies show that similar methods with students who would be considered to have mild reading disabilities have results of up to 80% of students no longer needing special education services. Think about the implications. What if 50% of all students in special education (taking the 80% of SLD students and adding a small error rate in the other categories that are "soft") do not actually have disabilities and actually just need intensive interventions?

The neuropsychology work by Sally Shawitz has shown very similar results and is worth examining if that topic interests you.

Is this really happening???

A snapshot of one district's data.... Percentage ELL qualified for special education by building

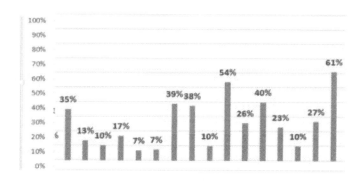

The graph above is from one of the school districts that Steve worked with on ELL and Special Education Issues. However, Steve has seen this same type of data across numerous districts, and for both ELL and non-ELL students. Some of this is caused by small data sets and how they can provide results that are more random than real. However, this type of pattern is common enough that the problem is beyond small sample size issues. Even after subtracting out small sample problems, this type of graph shows that whether or not a student qualifies for special education can change depending upon the school they are in at the time. This is more information to show staff that qualification rates do not equal disability rates.

Keeping Special Ed in Proportion, by Anthony Rebora, available at:
http://www.edweek.org/tsb/articles/2011/10/13/01disproportion.h05.html

> ... *African-American students were nearly or greater than twice as likely as white students to be classified with emotional or intellectual disabilities*

In other words, there are kids who are placed in these programs because educators either don't want to deal with them, don't know how to deal with them, or don't know how to be responsive to them.

Scholars generally don't blame racial disproportionality in special education on outright discrimination. Instead, they say it typically derives from systemic flaws within a school or district's instructional culture that allow for some disadvantaged students to fall through the cracks.

Our problems are not about bad people doing bad things, given educators are good and caring people doing their best. The poor results as noted in the quote prior and the following quote are about systems level flaws that usually can be traced back to unconscious bias (our acculturation and our belief systems) and a lack of knowledge (what to do differently).

This was during a report to congress.

Using data from the U.S. Department of Education, analyses suggest that Black children are 2.88 times more likely than White children to be labeled as having mental retardation and 1.92 times more likely to be labeled as having an emotional/behavioral disorder (Losen & Orfield, 2002). Research suggests that unconscious racial bias, stereotypes, inequitable implementation of discipline policies, and practices that are not culturally responsive may contribute to the observed patterns of identification and placement for many minority students."

Information from the *Twenty-fourth Annual Report to Congress on the Implementation of the Individuals with Disabilities Education Act (IDEA)* (U.S. Department of Education, 2002), available at: http://www2.ed.gov/about/reports/annual/osep/2002/index.html

The majority of referrals contain reading concerns

We know that reading is a primary or additional concern in the majority of special education referrals. Dr. Carnine's meta-analysis of RTI/MTSS work shows that 70%-90% of the students we would like to qualify for special education in the 2nd or 3rd grade are not in need of qualification after they receive appropriate interventions. The work of Dr. Torgesen and the research on Lindamood Bell work shows as high as 80% of the students with reading disabilities can be brought to grade level with short-term intense intervention. We know that in many, possibly most cases, special education services within any given district encumbers upon general education funding (special education does not get enough money to pay its own bills).

So, what if a large number of students could be brought to grade level with the appropriate early interventions or short term intense interventions? We would not only save money, we would also have students finding more success. We mentioned earlier that the three top-performing elementary schools in Kent have very low rates of special education qualification (and, these are not high SES schools). Also, a school district south of Kent was just recognized as having the fastest achievement gap closure in the state (they are also one of the only school districts using RTI as a districtwide method of special education qualification in Washington). These things cannot all be happening by chance!!!

The following information is taken from a presentation that Dr. Joseph Torgesen provided called "A Scientific Success Story: Specific Reading Disabilities or Developmental Dyslexia" at the Florida Council for Exceptional Children, October 2006.

Dr. Torgesen reported on an intensive intervention provided for 60 students who had severe reading disabilities. The children were between 8 and 10 years of age. They had been receiving special education services for an average of 16 months. They were considered the worst readers and were on average at least 1.5 S.D. below grade level. They had standard scores of 69 for Word Attack, 69 for Word Identification and had Verbal IQs of 93 (average for each of these). These students were randomly assigned to two different groups and explicitly taught phonics skills. Both groups of students received 67.5 hours of one-to-one instruction, 2 hours per day for 8 weeks. The students were followed for two years after the intervention was completed.

The results of the work are the following. The students not only gained skills that placed them in the average range, they actually continued to increase their reading skills after the intervention, scoring higher on standardized testing 2 years after the post intervention testing than at the post intervention testing. This means that they didn't just make initial gains, they didn't just maintain those gains, they improved relative to their peers over time.

Dr. Torgesen then asked the question, "How do we make this kind of instruction available to every child who needs it?" Imagine the positive impact on our children, both short-term and long-term, if we achieved this! Imagine the positive impacts on our classrooms if we achieved this!

9. Impact of Race on Qualification Rates

Does anyone still believe that people from different races have different rates of disabilities? When Steve was working on the over identification of Black/African American students as students with intellectual disabilities, he was told the following more than once: "Everyone knows that Black/African American students have lower average IQs, which means there will be more with IQs below 70, and that is why we have more qualified for Intellectual Disabilities." This is no joke, people really said that and believed that. Sadly, this type of thinking was exacerbated due to a book called The Bell Curve. This book provides data that people take out of context and use inappropriately. Also, it is the belief of this author that the authors of The Bell Curve do not understand what impacts intelligence test scores. Again, belief systems and acculturation have an impact on the way in which we see the world. For people who believe things like this, it is much easier for them to believe that their tests are an accurate representation if the results are poor (most of these people are good and caring people, just in need of some new knowledge). They are less likely to question their results and look for a different explanation/cause.

The quotes noted above show extreme disproportionality in our qualification rates of our Black/African American students. We say that we believe that the rate of disabilities does not differ by race, yet our qualification rates vary to the extreme for certain groups in certain categories. This is evidence that we need to examine our beliefs systems and acculturation. This is a complex topic, yet sincere and open conversations and reflection are needed to find our way to better results.

Matthew Ladner and Christopher Hammons argue that race plays an enormously important role in how students are identified as disabled (Ladner and Hammons, 2001). In a study in the book *Rethinking Special Education for a New Century,* they found that in districts with a predominantly Black faculty, there was a reduction in minority student enrollment in special education services by three to four times. "Race," they concluded, "impacts special education rates far more than any other variable."

This examination of special education was prepared for the Center for Public Education by Ulrich Boser, October 15, 2009, available at:

http://www.centerforpubliceducation.org/Main-Menu/Evaluating-performance/Special-education-At-a-glance/Special-education-A-better-perspective-full-report.html

On a related note: Is race even a valid construct? This is a topic for many to discuss, but not a topic for this book. The term race is being used in this book for two reasons. It is used in all districts, all states, and at the national level for separating the students into groups. There is disproportionality across some groups and not others and the patterns of disproportionality are consistent. This is the problem. Yet this construct, valid or not, helps you know where to focus your efforts, once you know your numbers.

One more related note is the discussion of cultural competency versus cultural responsiveness. As noted earlier, Steve usually uses Latino and Black. Someone asked Steve why he was doing this, questioning his cultural competence. In education, there has been a great effort to make people culturally competent, which is something Steve and others question. The concept of cultural competence is based on a belief that we can look at someone and tell by their appearance what culture they identify with and then apply our knowledge of that culture. Steve uses Latino, given that his Spanish teacher uses the term Latino. However, he has talked to many people who could be Latina, Hispanic, Cubano, Peruana, Chicano, … about this very topic. Roughly 40% of the people Steve talked to identified as Hispanic and 40% Latino, with 20% not identifying as either, but instead as Cubano, Peruana, Chicano, … Also, Steve uses Black instead of African American, because two of his sons identify as Black, and not African American. Steve knows this because he asked them, independently, and they explained why they identify as Black and not African American. Steve also asked a co-worker the same question, and she identified as African American and explained why.

The point of this discussion is that we cannot know the cultural identity of someone by simply looking at them. Furthermore, even if we could, there are at least 400+ cultures within our schools (we have over 400 languages in our schools and that translates into well over 400 cultures), and we could not possibly know specific details about every one of these groups (even if we could identify people by their appearance). Instead, we need to be culturally responsive. We need to be careful in watching the people we work with. We need to watch their body language, have the courage to tell people that we need their help in understanding their culture, and have the courage to tell people that we might make mistakes and that we want them to educate us.

Did this chapter on Belief Systems and Acculturation change the way you look at the following chart?

A snapshot of one district's data.... Percentage ELL qualified for special education by building

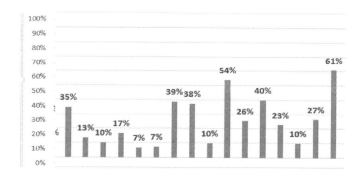

Do you now see that it is likely that the results are based upon inappropriate qualifications? Can you see yourself as part of the solution?

10. Qualification Does Not Equal Disability

The rate in which we qualify students for special education is far above the rate that there are actually students with disabilities. Here are some examples:

First, the research completed by Steve showed that districts with low qualfications rates had low F/R meal rates and districts with high qualification rates had high F/R meal rates, and there is no relationship that is meaningful between poverty and disability rates for our students.

The research by Steve Hirsch and the research by Walter Gilliam help us to see that our biases are impacting our work, making many of our decisions very subjective instead of objective, and impacting our results.

Other research shows profoundly different rates of qualification for our children of color, depending upon where they live. You cannot have a disability that appears and disappears depending upon your zip code.

Steve has data from over 1,500 school districts across 7 states and this data shows we are 48% more likely to qualify a language learner for special education than a native English speaker. There is nothing about being a language learner that increases the likelihood of a disability, but it clearly increases the likelihood of qualification. Furthermore, the vast majority of the disproportionality has existed in one category, SLD. There has been consistent disproportionality in SLI and DD, yet these categories have (within this data set) had less disproportionality.

The rate of qualification for a specific learning disability tripled from the 1970's (far exceeding impact from population growth), leveled off between 2000 and 2004, and has been dropping since 2004. This has occured while RTI/MTSS has increased.

The state of Washington is one of the last states to implement a state supported RTI/MTSS initiative (it is in the process of development during the writing of this 3rd edition and is still without implementation). Washington is one of the few states whose special education qualificition rate is increasing. It has increased almost every year since 2004. Interestingly enough, the trend line of this increase is very similar to the trend line of the increase of Latino students and ELL qualification.

In Ohio, they pay school districts for their students who recieve special education services based upon the category of special education they qualify under. Is it a coincidence that two of the categories that are farthest above the national average for qualification rate are in the highest payment group? And the category that is the farthest below the national average for qualification rate is in the lowest payment group?

All of these things simply cannot be happening by chance!

"Takeaways"

1) We See What We are Acculturated to See: Real world examples of acculturation creating a lens. **We each need to examine the impact of our acculturation on our belief systems, on our practices, on our results.**

2) Steve's Personal Educator Journey: Real world example of developing over time, gaining new knowledge, changing practices. **Self-examination can be painful, but we need to figure out what we don't know, combine that with our acculturation issues, and remain lifelong learners, painful as it will be at times.**

3) Steve Hirsh's and Walter Gilliam's Research: Research that shows the impact of our biases. **We all have biases, we need to examine how they are impacting our work, our results.**

4) Monolingual Nation: Real world examples that help us see what could be unrealistic expectations and/or a lack of reasonable expectations. **We expect our students, at times, to achieve very difficult tasks. Can we prove that we are creating structures that lead to good results for the vast majority of our students??? A student is not necessarily disabled if they are struggling in a system in which more than 20% of the students are struggling!!!**

5) Literacy and Intelligence: Knowledge to help us see things differently. **We need to have knowledge to determine how things are related and correlated or not. Without this, we can make judgments that have no validity.**

6) Poverty: Research that shows our results, and indicates biases. **This is more evidence that our biases, beliefs, and acculturation impact our results. The more we know about where our problems are, the better we can focus on fixing our problems.**

7) Qualification vs Disability: Research that shows our results do not follow logical patterns, nor our "spoken" beliefs. **We need to examine our results and the results in our district, in order to understand where to begin our introspection, and where and how to change our practices.**

8) Reading and Referrals: Research that indicates our system, results and beliefs have significant flaws. **There are methods out there that lead to different results. This shows us that many of the students we believe have disabilities are just not getting their needs met. What are we going to do?**

9) Race vs Disability: Research that shows our results, again, do not follow logical patterns, nor our "spoken" beliefs. **Again, our results do not match what we say that we believe. We need to examine our acculturation, belief systems and practices to achieve better results. No shame, no blame.**

10) Qualification Does Not Equal Disability. **We need to look at what we are doing. If our schools have a high rate of qualification, it is likely that we are putting students into special education who do not truly have disabilities, and this makes it more difficult for special education to have positive results. This does not mean they don't need help, just that special education is not the correct intervention.**

Closing Thoughts on Belief Systems

During the editing of this book, the question was asked, "How do you change what people believe?" As educators, we are caring individuals and lifelong learners. The problems, or poor results, within disproportionality are not occurring due to individuals purposefully doing harmful things to children. As educators see the impact of their actions or inactions in this area they will be highly motivated to change the results. Working on belief systems and acculturation, although painful at times, will be something that they do. Knowing that belief systems are a combination of acculturation and knowledge, educators will look for the knowledge they need (some of which can be found in Steve's and Ushani's books) and other information contained in the books of the many individuals we refer to within our books. Then, you can use the processes within Steve's and Ushani's books to change practices, which lead to changes in results.

John Hattie is possibly the leading expert in the world on what is and is not effective within educational strategies (Hattie's books, like Visible Learning, are powerful and useful books to own). An effect size of .4 is basically what is expected, the .9 is a very large effect size, and the 1.57 and 1.62 are extremely large effect sizes. The following are some examples found within his books or through Google searches:

-.34 for Mobility

-.02 for Summer Vacation

.19 for Co/Team Teaching

.47 for Small Group Learning

.53 for Scaffolding

.90 for Teacher Credibility

1.57 for Collective Teacher Belief

1.62 for Teacher Expectations of Student Performance

It is easy to see from this that beliefs have extremely powerful effects on our results. Also, having the knowledge, like that provided by Hattie, can sure save a lot of time, time that could be wasted on practices that are proven to have low impact on student learning.

Anthony Muhammad, author of several books, wrote the following in his book *Overcoming the Achievement Gap Trap*, "We cannot solve the problem until we look at it differently" (page 61) and "We cannot pursue equality when our value systems favor one group over another, especially when we lack the courage to even discuss the problem objectively" (page 75).

The work by Carol Dweck and her book on growth mindset versus fixed mindset is fantastic information for anyone in the process of evaluating and working on their own beliefs. It is also a great book for book study groups and the valuable discussions that can occur during book studies.

Also, our book Processing Perspectives: Examining Beliefs, Biases, and Reality Through Stories can assist in working on belief systems. The book provides real stories for educators, from educators, so that readers can examine and discuss a potentially different perspective.

You have seen the problems, the issues about acculturation and belief systems, their impact on practice and results. It will take courage and knowledge to move forward. The good news is that better results lead to higher levels of satisfaction, so it will be worth it.

Chapter 8: Special Education Categories - Problem areas

The reality is that most referrals lead to evaluations and most evaluations lead to qualification. This can be a good thing or this can be a bad thing. If your team has done a great job of evaluating your data, and the data shows proportional qualification and strong intervention systems (i.e., low % qualified for special education services and high test scores), then referrals leading to evaluations and to qualification (in most cases) means that your team is doing a great job in referring, testing, and qualifying the students who truly have disabilities that are adversely impacting their education and need something "special." Without that strong intervention and pre-referral process, your team is primarily guessing or assuming once it is time to make the decision regarding whether or not to qualify the student for special education services. Guessing might be strong language, but at the minimum the confidence of your team in its decisions will vary greatly.

The purpose of this chapter is to help you understand that the majority of disproportionality occurs within certain disability categories.

"Hard" Categories with Little or No Disproportionality

By any chance, are we evaluating a student who happens to possibly be eligible in one of the "hard" categories? The "hard" categories are the more concrete in nature and it is likely that neither language acquisition nor race nor poverty are a defining characteristic (when disproportionality exists). For example, children with blindness or deafness are highly likely to need special education services, and their race and/or linguistic history are unlikely to be defining or major factors in qualification or not.

Therefore, we are not including any extra discussion regarding these categories:

- Hearing Impairment or Deafness
- Visual Impairment (including Blindness)
- Orthopedic Impairment
- Traumatic Brain Injury
- Deaf-Blind
- Multiple Disabilities
- Autism

The category of Autism, in some regions, has had language specific disproportionality. Therefore, a quick look at your data in this category is advised.

Good news: the above categories represent at least 50% of the categories, sadly though not 50% of the students. Also, the determinant factor for these categories is almost always the disability, and the language acquisition is an additional factor.

Categories with an Interesting History, Yet Fewer Current Problems

The eligibility categories in this group are more difficult to analyze yet are not as extreme as the final categories. They are more difficult in this context due to the impacts of language learning, acculturation issues, poverty issues, and more. Additionally, historical issues of over-qualification of language learners and certain racial groups within intellectual disability might have impacted the way in which educators think about this category (i.e., some people might believe that certain groups have higher rates of intellectual disabilities).

- Other Health Impairment
- Intellectual Disability
- Emotional/Behavioral Disability

The category of Intellectual Disability, in some regions, has had language specific disproportionality. Therefore, a quick look at your data in this category is advised.

Other Health Impairment

The issue here tends to be under qualification for language learners. In many cases, this appears to be caused by the difficulties the families face in navigating our medical system and/or families in poverty could be struggling with medical coverage issues. These struggles often lead to under identification in this category. And, from what Steve has seen from many districts, the students who are struggling are then placed into the Specific Learning Disability category inappropriately in many cases.

The word "inappropriately" is used given that a service based upon a faulty qualification often does not align properly. In other words, the service is not addressing the core or root problem causing the delay. For example, if a student has ADHD and the ADHD is creating problems with learning to read or do math, that student might need the delivery of instruction modified to increase engagement. In contrast, a student who has similar delays that are caused by a learning disability is likely to need the content (materials) and/or methodology modified to increase learning.

This category tends to be easier in the terms of qualification, if one can get the needed documentation. It is important to note that the laws place the responsibility on the district to obtain any information that it believes necessary to appropriately qualify a student. That is a very tricky responsibility to navigate and staff really need to work with their administrative teams to travel that road.

If you have the needed documentation, the process is reasonably simple. In any of these cases, the team needs to determine the relationship between the noted condition, the adverse impact on the student to accessing their education (with and without language impact) and whether or not the student needs special education (specially designed instruction that is not dependent upon impacts of language acquisition) in order to access their education. If language learning was not an issue, would the medical condition by itself be creating this adverse impact? To the same extent?

Sadly, when teams do not know what to do, they may default to pushing these hard to identify students into the Specific Learning Disability category through inappropriate application of the legal term "professional judgment." If your team is facing this tough decision, there are ways to look at the data and come to a better decision.

Intellectual Disability for Language Learners

The category of intellectual disability used to be a problem area for language learners. The data I have seen over past years indicates that disproportionate qualification in this category is not as common as in the past. Your data needs to be examined for proportionality not just by language learner status, but also within each of the major language groups (the averaging effect can hide problems).

The cognitive testing of language learners is challenging. Our book *Lessons Learned* provides information to improve strategies.

In addition, adaptive behavior scales (necessary for considering Intellectual Disability qualification) are normed on what we believe is appropriate development in these areas (given the normative sample). In many cases you will get results that are either totally useless or of such questionable use that you cannot use them to determine if there are potential disability issues versus issues that are culturally based issues. Therefore, if you must use an adaptive behavior measure (and sometimes you are required to based upon the laws), you really need to get to know more about the exposure, experiences, expectations, and practice history of the student.

For example, for a student who is unable to (or just does not) feed themselves (according to the rating scale), have they ever been asked/required to do so? Or, for a student who cannot put on a jacket by themselves, did they live in an area in which the weather didn't require the use of jackets? Or, for a student who cannot tie their own shoes, do they have shoes without laces? Keep going with this line of logic for any question in which a student is not demonstrating a skill just in case they had limited exposure/experience/expectations/practice.

Then, start asking about the daily life of the student in their previous environment. It is possible you are going to find out that they can do something rather difficult that many students "here" could not do (e.g., start a fire without matches, hunt/fish with limited resources, etcetera). In the end, you must take into account the relationship of exposure/experience/expectation/practice to actual performance. It is unfair to consider a student impaired if they never had exposure/experience/expectation/practice with the skill, or that it was very limited. For example, considering a student to have fine motor issue with a pencil when they only just started to use one would be inappropriate. Also, it would be unfair to neglect the skills a student has but are not measured on our rating scales. In the end, though, the team will need to decide based on exposure/experience/expectations/practice: does this student actually have an impairment or not?

With students who potentially have intellectual disabilities or learning disabilities, and are language learners, intelligence testing is highly problematic. There really is no way to find an intelligence test that always works with students being considered in either of these categories. Some people believe that non-verbal intelligence testing solves these problems. However, that is just not true. For some of our students, a non-verbal intelligence test is much more likely to lead to accurate results. However, this method alone does not always solve the problem because the tests are designed and normed on our students who have grown up within the majority culture here in the United States. Therefore, some of our students who have not had the exposure and experience with the same types of toys and books (and environment) are at a competitive disadvantage when attempting these tests. The non-verbal intelligence tests often rely on picture analysis and predicting that can be practiced/strengthened through toys, games, puzzles. This leads to results that just cannot be trusted. In general, students do not get scores higher than they truly deserve, but there are a tremendous number of reasons why a student could achieve a score far lower than their actual ability level.

Emotional Behavioral Disability for Language Learners

Before referring a student for evaluation for Emotional Behavioral Disability, you need to be able to rule-out a lot of issues.

First, is the student's bad behavior (we would not be looking at this category if bad behavior was not present) actually the cause of the adverse impact on their access to their education? Or, is the lack of ability to communicate wants and needs creating bad behavior (due to frustration)? You are only going to be able to analyze this if you have the data very well documented for your school and district. In other words, how many of your ELL students are demonstrating problem behaviors and to what degree? What percentage of your ELL students are finding academic success? How does that rate compare to research on effective ELL programs (look into the work of Dr. Collier and Dr. Thomas, if you have not already done so)?

Second, is the student a student who needs support for trauma? If there is a history of trauma, and it is untreated, you might provide support for the student that is of little or no value. No quantity of the wrong intervention leads to good results.

Third, what is the relationship of academic struggles to the noted behavior? That is, if a student is behaving poorly to hide academic struggles, then the intervention needed is much different than if the bad behaviors are causing academic struggles.

Last, is there a cultural issue that is not being addressed? The majority of students qualified in this category are boys and some of our boys are coming from cultures that have a very different outlook in general and sometimes specifically in male/female power relationships. This is a difficult area to address, but we do not want to label a child as disabled due to struggles they are having with cultural differences.

Problem Categories for Language Learners and Disproportionality

The following categories have the largest disproportionality for language learners:

- Speech or Language Impairment
- Developmental Delay
- Specific Learning Disability

The categories of Speech or Language Impairment and Developmental Delay often have over qualification for our language learners, but it is usually not extreme. For example, the author often sees a district using SLI 10-12% of the time in general (within special education qualified students), and 14-16% of the time for special education students who are also ELL qualified students (within the subgroup of Special Education/ELL qualified students). In contrast, SLD is used at roughly 38.8% of all special education qualified students, but the author usually sees districts using this at 50-85% for the dually qualified students (within the subgroup of Special Education/ELL qualified students). And, SLD is the most difficult category to do correctly in general, and even more difficult to do correctly with our language learners.

Speech or Language Impairment

There are two main areas that create concerns: language (expressive and receptive) and articulation. Within the area of language, there are times in which grammar becomes an issue. This tends to ignore the information that exists on the development of language for a second or later language for the student. Even for students who are simultaneous bilinguals, usually one of the languages is not as strong as the other language and will continue to have some grammar issues, possibly throughout life. For students who are sequential bilinguals, mastering certain aspects of grammar may take a lifetime or just may not occur at all. For anyone who is learning Spanish, reaching a near 100% correct usage of "por" and "para" just might never occur. For someone coming from Spanish to English, mastering when to use "in" versus "on" can take a lifetime. I am using the English and Spanish examples given my experience with them, but also because 75% of our ELLs are Spanish to English learners (at last check this was 64% in Washington, 82% in California, and 90% in Texas).

When an SLP is considering a student for qualification in the category of Speech or Language Impairment, they need to have a strong knowledge of the student's language acquisition history and knowledge about that language within the community. In Steve's experience across many districts, a certain pattern occurs: not all of the languages are represented within the special education student group, and for some languages, students are only qualified in those "hard" categories. For example, the Kent School District normally has 130 to 140 languages spoken. However, we usually only have 40-45 of those languages represented within our special education student population. This is, in part, due to sample sizes (some of the languages only have 1-2 speakers and you should not expect to see a student within all of those groups).

However, that does not explain the size of the difference. Also, some languages are over-represented and the patterns of the over-representation are consistent. Spanish tends to be over represented for language (expressive and receptive) and some Asian languages are over represented for articulation. So, once a therapist knows this information, they can then talk to people about the usage of the language in the community (especially for the high incidence languages). A key issue is whether or not the student in question for qualification for language services actually needs English when they leave the school setting (or even needs it within the school setting). For example, can the student travel within the school or community and only use very little English? If this is the case, then the apparent needs/adverse impact of the student in English would need to be extreme to justify qualification, and, the student would need to demonstrate significant issues within their native language (according to multiple speakers of that language). Without this, we would be qualifying students simply because they do not practice something that really is not that important in their life: English. Additionally, their exposure might be limited within and outside the school.

What about articulation? The therapist really needs to know about the structure of the language, whether or not the sounds of English are present within the language of the student, and the developmental norms for that language. It is inappropriate to qualify a student for articulation issues when the sounds that are creating the problematic score do not exist in the primary language of the student or are not yet developmentally expected in the student's native language.

The following charts are used by SLPs to help parents understand the developmental ages related to sounds/blends, the first chart is for English and the second for Spanish. Trying to find this same information for other languages becomes more difficult as the languages become less commonly used. Additionally, after reading several of books on this, I have found out some of the content is highly inaccurate. And, we have over 400 languages spoken in our schools in the United States. It takes work to find out the developmentally appropriate ages and the differences in sounds across these 400+ languages, but that is needed to know whether or not your evaluation of the student has any validity or usefulness.

English

Developmental Articulation Norms –

AGES

4	5	7	7.5	8.5
m	k	v	r	z
h	g	-ing	l	th (the)
n	d		s	th (with)
w	f		ch	
b	y		sh	
p	t		j	
			/r/ blends	
			/s/ blends	
			/l/ blends	

Based on: Massachusetts Speech and Hearing Association Entrance and Exit Criteria Guidelines
90% mastery

Spanish

Developmental Articulation Norms –

AGES

3	4	5	6	7
m	k	d	x	rr
b	l	g	s	
p	w	ñ		
	f	r		
	y	ch		
	t			
	n			

Based on: Jimenez 1987, Acevedo 1993
90% mastery

Developmental Delay for Language Learners

The category Developmental Delay consists of five subcategories: Social or Emotional, Adaptive, Communication, Cognitive and Motor (Physical Development).

This category could be the category in which exposure/experience/expectations/ practice are the most critical. You will be trying to determine whether or not a young child/student who could be coming to you from poverty with language differences, and probably cultural differences, has a disability that impacts their access to their general daily activities. The Preschool Version of the ELL Critical Data Process focuses on understanding these issues for preschool age language learners. In the end, your team will need to determine whether or not, regardless of the score, the student had a real opportunity to grow the skill in question like a student who was within the normative sample. Remember that the category Developmental Delay is a category of special education. Therefore, the team may indicate a belief that the student is likely to have a disability, which may be accurate, or that the delay may respond to intervention (meaning no disability).

Exposure, Experience, Expectations and Practice must be examined.

Social/emotional issues: The team must integrate their information from before (or possibly during the referral process) to their data obtained during the evaluation process if an evaluation is recommended and completed. Based on that information, can the team state that social-emotional issues exist to the extent that, after subtracting out issues with exposure/experience/ expectations/ and/or practice, there would still be a large enough problem/concern.

Adaptive behavior: When the team is looking at adaptive behavior, they must go through a similar process, answering the same basic questions. Additionally, they must be able to come to the conclusion that, after subtracting out language and culture (if there are applicable issues), the student would still have significant impacts within adaptive behavior that are directly, or primarily, related to a potential disability. A major hurdle for teams to overcome during this process is the belief that they must provide special education as the early intervention. The issue or problem here is that they are stating that the child has a disability. They are not stating on the report, under qualification, that they "just want to help." Chapter 9 has an activity used to generate alternative ideas to this practice.

A child cannot, should not, be qualified as having a disability simply because a family cannot or will not create the needed experiences, exposure, expectations and then support these with practice. When the presenting problem does not represent a disability, the problem is better solved through working with the families or communities to create the needed experiences, exposure, expectations and practice. This is not a value judgment. Many families are doing their very best to provide food and shelter.

Specific Learning Disability

Specific Learning Disability (SLD) is the category with the highest degree of disproportionality for our language learners. Also, it is the hardest category to do correctly with our language learners. That is a bad combination.

This is a category that was, more or less, created for the special education world. After this was first found in the special education laws, in 1975, they did not even have a method to measure it. What became known as the discrepancy model has been found to have significant flaws. It is likely that the discrepancy model is roughly as accurate as flipping a coin, possibly less accurate. Specific Learning Disability is the only category that greatly increased beyond population change from 1975 to 2004, when the special education population in the United States "peaked" between 2000 and 2004. It is the main category to decrease in size since 2004. The SLD category tripled in numbers from 1975 to 2004, eventually being the category in which roughly 50% of all special education students were qualified. Interestingly enough, the decrease in this category started with the federal law that included the usage of RTI qualification. It is easy to see the decrease in the SLD category aligning with the increased usage of RTI within the school systems. Although it should be simple to state the exact percentage of the students qualified in this category, it just isn't. As of the day that I typed this sentence in 2020, I found one website (official government sites) stating 33.6% and another stating 38.8%. It is safe to state, also using the data I have seen from hundreds of districts, that the percentage is in the mid-thirties. Always check multiple sources. Within my own state they had ELL statistics that were completely different because they were calculating two different things but using the same label.

Throughout this book there are quotes regarding the work by Dr. Carnine and Dr. Torgesen that speak to the problems with this category. Also, the work by Steve regarding poverty and qualification, most of which occurs in this category, adds to the evidence that this is our most problematic category.

As noted in the law, school teams are supposed to have practices that do not lead to discrimination, and school teams are supposed to evaluate the student in the student's native language (or using a format most likely to yield accurate information). Yet, we know that our practices lead to the use of the SLD category at rates higher for our ELL students (sometimes much higher). And, for our language learners we are saying that these students have a disability in reading, math or written language in a language they are just learning (unless we have proof that they had the same learning issues in their prior country when applicable).

For students who potentially have intellectual disabilities and potentially have learning disabilities, and are also language learners, intelligence testing is highly problematic. There really is no way to find an intelligence test that always works with students being considered in either of these categories. Some people believe that non-verbal intelligence testing solves these problems. However, that just is not true. For some of our students, a non-verbal intelligence test is much more likely to lead to accurate results. However, as noted earlier, this method alone does not always solve the problem because the tests are designed and normed on our students who have grown up within the majority culture here in the United States. Therefore, some of our students who have not had the exposure and experience with the same types of toys and books (and environment) are at a competitive disadvantage when attempting these tests. This leads to results that just cannot be trusted. In general, students do not get scores higher than they truly deserve, but there are a tremendous number of reasons why a student could achieve a score far lower than their actual ability level.

The following law brings into question several more problem areas with our students who might be considered as potentially having a specific learning disability.

WAC 392-172A-03040

"(2)(a) A student **must not be determined to be eligible** for special education services **if** the determinant factor is:

(i) **Lack of appropriate instruction in reading**, based upon the state's grade level standards;

(ii) **Lack of appropriate instruction in math**; or

(iii) **Limited English proficiency**; and

(b) If the student does not otherwise meet the eligibility criteria including presence of a disability, adverse educational impact and need for specially designed instruction.

(3) In interpreting evaluation data for the purpose of determining eligibility for special education services, each school district must:

(a) Draw upon information from a variety of sources, including aptitude and achievement tests, parent input, and teacher recommendations, as well as information about the student's physical condition, social or cultural background, and adaptive behavior; and

(b) **Ensure that information obtained from all of these sources is documented and carefully considered.**"

Bold and underlining added for emphasis.

This law has several issues that apply to evaluation. School teams are supposed to rule-out lack of appropriate instruction in reading and math. However, how does a student get appropriate instruction in reading and math if that instruction is not provided in their native language? School teams are supposed to factor in social and cultural background yet in most evaluations it is very difficult to find evidence of this done with fidelity. Is there appropriate instruction in reading and/or math if less than 50% of the students are passing the state tests? 40%? 30%? 20%? How has language acquisition and language level been accounted for in a meaningful way?

You have seen the problems and concerns, now what?

We suggest introspection, examining data, using a process, monitoring the results, and adjusting to meet goals that represent proportionality. This is not about putting fewer kids into special education (if your numbers already make sense), and it is also not about putting more kids in either (we are already over identifying). It is about qualifying the right kids. This is hard to do, unless you and your team work to identify the issues and address them.

From section 3(b) above: **Ensure that information obtained from all of these sources is documented and carefully considered."**

During the trainings, Steve uses real evaluation reports from each of the regions. From this, Steve has been provided well over 300 evaluation reports and estimates that he has seen roughly 70-80% that have ZERO data regarding the impact of language acquisition, about 20% that don't even note the student is a language learner or speaks another language, and only a few that have some information directly related to how they determined determinant factor. The law requires that we not only have multiple sources of data, but that we carefully consider all sources and document these sources. In discussing this with educators across the country this is not occurring due to a lack of care or effort, but instead due to a lack of training. Within this book, our book *Lessons Learned While Evaluating ELL Students for Potential Special Education Qualification,* and our workbook is the information needed and examples needed to integrate this type of information into the evaluation reports.

Chapter 9: Core Instruction, then proof, then potential intervention if needed

Core Instruction

Over the course of doing 15 years of professional training on ELL and Special Education issues, I have received many questions regarding intervention. It took me many years to learn to change the discussion. Before we can talk about intervention, we must first know whether or not any core instruction has occurred. Then, we need to know whether or not the core instruction worked, who did it work for, who did it not work for. Then, if we find, via proof, that our core instruction is working for the vast majority of students, we can talk about interventions.

During the writing of this 3rd edition, some of the most common questions/statements, related to this issue, were presented to Steve during consultation. Here are three of them, and you should try to figure out the flaw for each question before reading the following paragraphs:

1) He/she couldn't learn how to _____ until we used an interpreter.
2) There are so many language learners with memory/processing issues.
3) So many of the kids from _____ country/language are having a really hard time learning.

In number 1, the student didn't have a learning problem. If I were to have someone teach you a new computer skill speaking to you in Russian (for those of you who don't speak/read Russian) and the keyboard and screen were in Russian, you would also struggle to "learn." It isn't about a learning problem regarding computer skills, nor a disability.

In number 2, the simple fact that a student is a language learner doesn't increase the likelihood of a processing or memory issue. Folks can argue anywhere from .5% to 5% of students have issues in these areas that are significant enough to cause learning problems. Therefore, it isn't "so many!" It is between 1 in 20 and 1 in 200. The fact is, what is often referred to a "memory" problem or a "processing" problem, is actually a language problem. It is really hard to remember or process something that was explained in a language you didn't understand or didn't fully understand.

In number 3, there is no country or language where learning problems based upon a disability occur at a higher rate. So, like in number 2, it should be rare and not the norm. There will be some argument to this when the students are coming from a region with a known and higher rate of a specific medical issue. Bring the proof, before bringing the opinion, though.

Ready means never…*

In the real world, sometimes we will need to talk about interventions before we fix the problems of a lacking or non-existent core instruction. However, long-term success relies on focusing on the core instruction and the success of the core instruction before completing interventions with students who did not respond well to instruction that was powerful for the majority of the students. When a team starts, it might find that 0% of students are successful in the core instruction (a real example from a discussion that occurred the week prior to writing this). It is possible that only 20%-30% are successful with the core instruction (also real example and not uncommon, just check the district report cards on the state education website). It could be that 80% are successful, and then we can dive deeply into the discussion of intervention. So, if you must complete an activity that is more aligned with interventions, prior to working on "core" issues, what is your 1 year, 3 year, and 5 year plan to reverse this trend and ensure strong core instruction? The "ready means never" has an asterisk because a famous educator used to always say that and I cannot find their name and do not actually know if they coined the phrase. But, in most actions, folks will hesitate to change until they are "ready" which leads to never changing.

Additionally, interventions are not synonymous with something to buy, a prepackaged program. Interventions can be about changing the focus or the intensity of existing programs. Also, interventions can be as simple as some creative thinking. We had a student who was missing a lot of school and found out that she had to get up and ready for school after her mother had left for work. Then, with some questioning, we found out that she was hitting the snooze button on her alarm clock until it didn't ring anymore. The intervention was her moving the alarm clock out of reach. The simple fact of her having to get up to turn it off solved the problem. So, you have a team of dedicated educators, be creative.

Bring your proof…

In order to know whether or not core instruction is working, you need to have your data. This needs to be proof, not feelings. A beginning to this for our ELL students can be the following (via a public records request to the state department of education):

For every district within the state and the state as a whole (individual school if possible) know at least the following:

1) What percentage of students are qualified for special education (school, district, state)?
2) What percentage of the ELL students are qualified for special education (school, district, state)? Don't confuse this with the reverse, the percentage of special education students ELL qualified.
3) What percentage of the students qualified speak only English?
4) What percentage of the ELL students have passed all levels of the language acquisition testing at 5.0 years (school, district, state)?
5) What are the test scores on the state reading and math testing for ELL students by language acquisition level (school, district, state)?

6) What percentage of the ELL students are qualified for gifted and talented services (school, district, state)?

You will need to know your district data for students passing the state reading and math testing for non-language learners (and if you have a large ELL population, remove them from the data to calculate this and then calculate the performance within their group).

It is difficult or impossible to call something an intervention when the skill either was not taught, or the rate of success within the population is low. Intervention discussion should be focused on what to do if a student hasn't been learning a skill within an environment in which learning the skill is the norm. And, for our ELL students that requires knowing how well our ELL students are doing within our setting.

Core Instruction, again

Within many, maybe most, districts there are students who are LTELs, long-term ELLs. This is occurring because the system has not been designed correctly to provide them the support and/or additional support that they need in order for them to be successful as a group. As noted above, I recently had a conversation with a teacher who told me that their school believed that the ELL students had reading disabilities. I asked how many ELL students she served, and the answer was 16. Then, I asked how many were being referred, the answer was 16. There is a chance that this is true, meaning they ALL have disabilities in reading, and that chance is about 1 in a quintillion (i.e., million, billion, trillion, quadrillion, quintillion). Literally, no joke!

Therefore, if you are in a situation in which the majority or an entire group of students, all language learners, at about the third-fourth grade are being referred for special education services and all for the same concerns, then there is a really good chance that the problem is a systems level problem. In other words, we need to figure out the core issues these students are struggling with and provide additional services in those areas. It is possible that some educators will call these interventions, but it is difficult to call something an intervention that either has not been taught, has not been taught effectively, or for some reason just has not been learned. This is not to place blame, neither on the educators, nor on the students (which has been the traditional route, given the significant over qualification for special education services). Instead, this is about getting people to look at the problem differently and begin to solve the problem with a different approach. Special education should not continue to be "the only game in town."

The following paragraphs include a different approach for the K-12 levels and the preschool levels. Later in this book there are additional specific interventions/practices examples for students as related to specific information discovered during the ELL Critical Data Process.

Chapter and LAP services for designing ELL

In working with teams across the country, it became painfully apparent that the number one activity that I have been told about regarding ELL services is class work and homework assistance. As noted above, this does not align with the expectations, nor what "we" are getting the money for regarding ELL qualified students. However, a sad reality is that the funds for our language learners are rather meager and it is very difficult to build programs based upon the funding model. The following is one example of using existing resources to create a program for language learners that would focus on listening, speaking, reading and writing.

This is based upon taking the materials that already exist for Chapter and/or LAP services and changing the focus or simply increasing the emphasis on the listening, speaking, reading and writing in relationship to a language learner and language development.

The services that exist are designed to teach struggling readers to improve their reading skills. It is very common for these materials to be picture rich. Therefore, the ELL service provider could take the same materials and first focus on listening. The provider could discuss the picture(s) by pointing to different parts, naming the parts and naming the actions that are occurring. Then, the provider could read the materials to the children and ask questions. The children would have had exposure to the pictures and the reading that is related to the pictures. The children should be allowed to answer in their native language or in English (an iPhone or iPad might be needed to assist with voice translation). As times goes on, this would be used less and less. This activity, as a starting point, would allow the students to work on listening and speaking. Then, after 2-3 trials with the same materials, the students would be paired up and would read the materials to each other. Then, students would have specific questions they would need to ask their partners. Last, in this section, the students would report to the group about: 1) What they learned, 2) What they liked, 3) and What they imagine could happen next if the story were to continue.

The act of writing is extremely difficult in a new language. Taking the above materials after the multiple trials, I would first want students to write a correct answer (single word) within a blank space (but, I would have a word bank with the correct answers). This would be followed by the students using sentence starters, and eventually writing on practiced materials without assistance.

This is just a short description of what can be done. The hope of this idea is that a team would read this idea and run with all the possible additions that could be made that would focus, in a language developmentally appropriate manner, on the areas of listening, speaking, reading and writing.

Preschool activity

At the preschool level, the staff I have worked with throughout my career are many of the most loving and caring individuals I have worked with in education. Teaching preschool takes a special kind of person. Knowing this, I know that every time I teach the preschool process I will face the same question/statement--- "Do you expect me to do nothing? How can I do nothing?" The belief, per se, is that qualification for special education is the only possible route to solving the problems. However, special education qualification requires the identification of a disability. Special education, "... is not a remedial service..." as stated within the handbook for the Iowa State Department of Education on special education evaluations.

This still leaves the teams with, "What do I do?"

During the training on the Preschool Version of the ELL Critical Data Process we do the following activity, an activity that could easily be done in every district. I provide the group the following examples of things that could be done in place of special education qualification, or before agreeing to a special education evaluation, to determine whether or not the student simply needed the correct exposure, experience, expectations and practice.

Home study packets

Training parents on setting up play dates

Parent training on interventions/practice

Grant for educational books and toys

Helping parents to arrange low cost and free medical (without questions...)

Providing parents information regarding co-op daycares

RTI groups (drop in)

Drop-In to existing programs (without qualification)

Parent Groups

Parent Liasons

Literacy classes for larger language groups (with free books)

We spend 2-3 minutes going over what each of these might look like. Then, people work in groups of 5-6 and they are to take 5 minutes to come up with as many additional ideas as they can.

At the end of the 5 minutes it is not uncommon for us, as an entire group, to now have 20-30 ideas. We talk about which of the ideas could be implemented almost immediately, which would take some time to implement (2-3 months) and which could take the next year to implement. The educators within the group usually see the items differently; however, each person is able to see several items they could implement immediately, several that would take some time, and some that would take longer. This allows everyone to have something they can do that replaces the feeling/need to qualify students for special education regardless of whether or not they have a disability. It is important to acknowledge that you might still be qualifying some students in a questionable manner as you increase the implementation of ideas like these. However, the harder you work on these ideas, the less likely that will be to occur. And, it is a fantastic feeling to create systems like these.

Interventions

For something to be an intervention, in this type of discussion, we should have already provided direct instruction, opportunity, exposure to the desired skill and/or behavior. Then, if we have a student whose data indicates they are not responding as well as students usually respond, we can then examine interventions. Later in the book there is discussion of interventions, and sometimes this line gets very blurry. That is OK. If this was easy, there would be a solution manual for any and all problems. The following are two examples of interventions related to information discovered during the ELL Critical Data Process discussions.

Parent Literacy in Primary Language

You have found out that the parents are not literate in the language they share with their child. If you already have a program for all language learners that is focused on listening, speaking, reading and writing, you can work to determine the vocabulary of this specific student. If you find that they have a level of vocabulary below what is average within your language learner group, you can work to build their vocabulary. In doing this, you could determine which of the most commonly used words in English that they have not yet mastered and first focus on building those words (given they are the building block for future learning). Then, you could examine from kindergarten and moving forward by grade which of the Common Core words they have not mastered and focus on those by grade level.

If your district really wants to take on a larger, yet amazing, project they could begin a Spanish literacy program for the parents. Within this program, with grant funding, the parents could be taught to read kindergarten and first grade level books (something they would need explanation for regarding the reasoning, using Stephen Krashen's comprehensible input as the reasoning). Then, as their skills grow, they could start reading these books to their children.

Rate of Growth on the State Language Acquisition Test

You have a program in place that is working for the vast majority of your students, but your data shows you that one subgroup of your language learners is not benefitting from the instruction as designed. Your team can analyze the issues and try to determine what the common issue/problem is for the students. This might involve "phoning a friend." The team then might discover that this group of students has cultural or environmental issues that are competing with what you are trying to teach. For example, the families may believe that our schooling and English are not truly important, but their language is very important. You discover that these students, with just a very small quantity of direct instruction, are reading at appropriate levels within their native language.

As an intervention, your team could meet with leaders within this group and seek to understand the issues at a deeper level. Then, work with the group to discuss the advantages of becoming bilingual or multi-lingual. Discuss the possible advantages these students would have, discuss the research regarding cognitive development for bilingual and multi-lingual individuals. Focus on the advantages and how these leaders might be able to help your school create a new narrative for the students that includes the value of successfully completing their new school experience.

The following is a short list of individual student interventions that educators took on because they wanted to be part of the solution:

- Small group reading or individual reading (anyone with expertise… be part of the solution)

- 5 Minute Artic from speech and language pathologists

- The two high school math teachers and a real pre-algebra class

- Math flash cards for automaticity when long-division struggles occur

- Individual reading tutoring in Spanish, with emphasis on transference of skills

- 1-to-1 behavioral coaching (specific work on concrete skills and positive connection with home for implementation of new learning)

Summary

We need to understand whether or not our system is working for our students, based upon proof. If we have groups of students who are not getting language learner instruction as it is meant to be (listening, speaking, reading, and writing), we need to figure out first how to achieve this instruction. Then, if our students are successful in general within this system, but there is a student (or a group of students) who is not successful, what do we do to help them? That is where the intervention work begins. And, the better this work is done, the easier it is to determine if a particular student's struggle is related to language learning or to language learning with a disability.

Appendix A: Sources of Information on Problems in Qualification and Disproportionality

Many of you will be facing a variety of challenges in discussing the appropriate students to evaluate for special education services. You are likely to face a lot of "push back" from your teams. This is due, in part, to people wanting to help children and not seeing other options. Part of convincing people of the necessity of looking for other options involves helping them to understand that the current option is not appropriate for some of our students. That is, if you have disproportionality (and almost everyone does), then some students are not getting the appropriate interventions. The following quotes are meant to help in the creation of new knowledge.

Each of these is directly quoted from the source noted. The source of the information for the following excerpts is listed first. Please refer to the source for further information.

ChildTrends

Child Trends Databank. (2014). Learning disabilities. Available at:
http://www.childtrends.org/?indicators=learning-disabilities

> *Differences by Parental Education In 2013, children who had a parent with a Bachelor's degree or higher were less likely to have a learning disability than those with parents who had only a high school diploma or some college…*

> *Children in poverty and in families that receive public assistance are more likely to be identified as having a learning disability.*

Authors' note: What is likely to be the real issue? We suggest the real issue here is that in many cases the students who are overqualified are lacking some of the exposure, experience, expectations and practice, instead of being students with disabilities. As noted earlier, what if the difference between proportional and disproportional is more about us the educators than it is about the students?

Education Week

Keeping Special Ed in Proportion, by Anthony Rebora, available at:
http://www.edweek.org/tsb/articles/2011/10/13/01disproportion.h05.html

> *… African-American students were nearly or greater than twice as likely as white students to be classified with emotional or intellectual disabilities*

> *In other words, there are kids who are placed in these programs because educators either don't want to deal with them, don't know how to deal with them, or don't know how to be responsive to them.*

> *Scholars generally don't blame racial disproportionality in special education on outright discrimination. Instead, they say it typically derives from systemic flaws within a school or district's instructional culture that allow for some disadvantaged students to fall through the cracks.*

Authors' note: What is likely occurring here? The authors suggest that acculturation and a lack of certain knowledge is impacting the decision makers in subtle ways, ways in which they are not aware. They need to see their own data and have some tough conversations to address these problems.

Report to Congress

Information from the *Twenty-fourth Annual Report to Congress on the Implementation of the Individuals with Disabilities Education Act (IDEA)* (U.S. Department of Education, 2002), available at:
http://www2.ed.gov/about/reports/annual/osep/2002/index.html

> *Using data from the U.S. Department of Education, analyses suggest that Black children are 2.88 times more likely than White children to be labeled as having mental retardation and 1.92 times more likely to be labeled as having an emotional/behavioral disorder (Losen & Orfield, 2002). Research suggests that unconscious racial bias, stereotypes, inequitable implementation of discipline policies, and practices that are not culturally responsive may contribute to the*

observed patterns of identification and placement for many minority
students.

Authors' note: What is likely occurring here? Like the authors of this quote said, there is unconscious bias and practices that are not culturally responsible. However, most people will struggle to see this and first need to see their own data to encourage introspection. This can be very hard to hear for the majority group. We need to have the courage for this introspection. It would be wonderful if similar research was occurring in the language acquisition world, but it is rare. During my career and especially during the past 10 years of working with educators from across the country, there is a clear disconnect between language learner services as designed for listening, speaking, reading and writing versus actual practice. In other words, practices that are not "linguistically responsible."

NASP (National Association of School Psychologists)

NASP Communiqué, Vol. 38, #1, September 2009

Multicultural Affairs, Confronting Inequity in Special Education, Part I: Understanding the Problem of Disproportionality, by Amanda L. Sullivan, Elizabeth A'Vant, John Baker, Daphne Chandler, Scott Graves, Edward McKinney, & Tremaine Sayles:

> *Black students, particularly those identified as mentally retarded or emotionally disabled, have been consistently overrepresented for more than 3 decades. Native American students are also persistently overrepresented in special education nationally, and while the same is not true for Latino students, they are often overrepresented at the state and district levels where their enrollment is highest.*

> *Special education identification patterns vary both between and within states. For instance, risk for Black students identified as mentally retarded is more than 14 times that of their White peers in some states while risk is nearly equivalent in others.*

> *The disproportionality literature tends to focus on the disability categories of mental retardation, learning disabilities, and emotional disabilities, as these are the high-incidence disabilities and constitute over 63% of students eligible for special education (U.S. Department of*

Education [USDOE], 2009). These are also widely regarded as "judgmental" categories because of relatively vague federal and state disability definitions that necessitate a high degree of professional judgment in making normative comparisons to determine eligibility (Klingner et al., 2005). This has led many to question the validity of these diagnoses as true disabilities and the likelihood of misidentification, particularly in light of the wide variation in identification rates across states and districts. In contrast, diagnoses in the low-incidence categories are rarely challenged because of their physical/medical bases, and because disproportionality is not generally observed in these categories.

Authors' note: What is likely occurring here? The authors want to focus on one portion of this quote that is often forgotten or overlooked. Is it possible to have a disability that appears and disappears depending upon your zip code? No way! Therefore, we need to remember that there are some significant issues regarding how subjective our practices are in these areas. Now, with data, we can work to become more objective. This is not bad people doing bad things, but instead poor practices leading to bad results. We need new practices and new knowledge to get new results. We either created or sustained the bad results, now we can solve the problems and achieve positive results.

Center for Public Education

This examination of special education was prepared for the Center for Public Education by Ulrich Boser, October 15, 2009, available at:

Found at: www.centerforpubliceducatio.org

The complete URL is listed below:

http://www.centerforpubliceducation.org/Main-Menu/Evaluating-performance/Special-education-At-a-glance/Special-education-A-better-perspective-full-report.html

The disparities between whites and some minorities in special education appear mostly in the categories with the most subjective eligibility criteria, such as "mild mental retardation" or "specific learning disabilities." Many believe the disproportionate representation is due to misconceptions about race and culture, and that Black and Hispanic children are more likely to be misidentified as disabled (Education Week 2004, National Research Council 2002).

For instance, Matthew Ladner and Christopher Hammons argue that race plays an enormously important role in how students are identified as disabled (Ladner and Hammons, 2001). In a study in the book Rethinking Special Education for a New Century, they found that in districts with a predominantly Black faculty, there was a reduction in minority student enrollment in special education services by three to four times. "Race," they concluded, "impacts special education rates far more than any other variable.

Authors' note: What is likely occurring here? If the rate in which students are qualified for special education varies in relationship to the race/ethnicity of the teachers, we really need to be willing to look at how our acculturation, knowledge and resulting belief systems are impacting our work. If we are the problem, then we can be the solution. We are loving and good people.

University of Texas at Austin

Education and Transition to Adulthood, Information on Learning Disabilities, available at: http://www.utexas.edu/cola/etag/Related%20Sites/Learning-Disabilities.php

Although the research focus has primarily been on the disproportionate labeling of racial minorities with LD, the research team found that differences in the rates of being labeled are more dramatic by socioeconomic status (SES) than by race. The odds of being labeled with LD are much higher among low SES than high SES high school students, regardless of whether the student is Black or white. In fact, low SES white high school students are as likely as low SES Black or Hispanic high school students to be labeled with LD, but much greater proportions of racial minorities are in that high-risk low SES group.

In contrast to Black and white high school students, high SES Hispanic high school students are as likely as low SES Hispanic high

school students to be labeled with LD. The team found that disproportionate labeling of Hispanic students with learning disabilities in high school is attributable to the over-labeling of language minorities.

The team also found that students attending higher poverty schools are actually less likely to be labeled with LD, and that systematic differences in academic achievement by SES, race, and linguistic status are a major factor in disproportionality.

Authors' note: What is likely occurring here? Mathematically there is only a tiny relationship between a student's parents being in poverty (putting the student into poverty) and the possibility that the parent and then the student will have a disability. However, the research is showing poverty as a very high predictor of whether or not a student will be qualified for special education services. Knowing this, each of us needs to understand whether or not this problem is occurring in our school district. Then, if it is occurring, we need to have conversations with everyone involved. Poverty does not create disabilities, but we might be labeling it as such. Use this information to help everyone move to better practices.

Appendix B: Recommended Books

Catherine Collier:

- Separating Difference from Disability

Virginia Collier and Wayne Thomas:

- Dual Language Education for a Transformed World
- Educating English Language Learners for a Transformed World

Carol Dweck

- Mindset: The New Psychology of Success

Steve Gill and Ushani Nanayakkara

- Lessons Learned While Evaluating ELL Students for Potential Special Education Qualification
- Evaluating ELL Students for the Possibility of Special Education
- Special Education Referral or Not
- ELL Teachers and Special Education
- Language Acquisition: Building a solid foundation and pursuing a new level of language mastery (Booklet)
- Processing Perspectives: Examining Beliefs, Biases, and Reality Through Stories
- The ELL Special Education Evaluation Workbook: Companion and Training Document for the ELL Critical Data Process

John Hattie

- Visible Learning: A Synthesis of over 800 Meta-Analyses Related to Achievement

Janet Klingner et al

- English Language Learners: Differentiating Between Language Acquisition and Learning Disabilities. *Council for Exceptional Children*

Appendix C: Using the ELL Critical Data Process for Interventions, Referrals, or Special Education Evaluations

This appendix is designed to provide a few examples of how the data could be used to design interventions, support a referral for special education services or support a special education evaluation. The discussions that occur during the ELL Critical Data Process are not meant to simply figure out where to put the check mark, the discussions should lead the team to ideas for areas in which to create interventions or to data needed to support the processing of a special education referral. And if the team proposes a special education evaluation (and the parents' consent), some of this data is needed to increase the likelihood of an accurate evaluation of a language learner.

The authors have seen where too much information leads teams into trying to fit their situation into a box, in place of using the examples to help guide. Therefore, in this section, we only provide some examples to provoke thought.

For many of the items, the discussion under Referral and Evaluation will be very similar. That is, in most cases you and your team are trying to decide if the weight of the evidence across many points supports a referral, and possibly at a later date whether the weight of the items, when combined with assessment data, supports a disability. If the student has a clear disability that is rarely impacted by language learning (i.e., the determinant factor is the disability and not the lack of English language acquisition), then these discussions are rather easy. This is the case for disabilities like blindness, deafness, and severe intellectual disabilities (what appears to be a mild intellectual disability could be something else, though). The majority of the problems, when teams will struggle most, are in the "soft" categories like specific learning disability, speech or language impairment, and developmental delay. Therefore, if any of these categories is the possible outcome of an evaluation, the data needs to be stronger and more clear-cut, given the disability determination is not.

K-12 Version

Item number 1: Students Primary Language Characteristics

Intervention: If the student is a Spanish speaking student, and lives in a community in which they can easily speak Spanish the vast majority of the time, it is likely that they need interventions that are designed to increase their vocabulary. Also, since they might not have any formal education in Spanish and may not be reading in Spanish, they may need vocabulary development in both English and Spanish.

If the student speaks a language other than English, and you have a specific example of them struggling with a skill that many students who speak that language and are learning English struggle with, the team needs to create an intervention that targets the specific concern. For many students who speak Asian languages, there is over qualification for speech and language services in the area of articulation. In place of special education qualification, the SLP could use the 5 Minute Artic method and do this as an RTI service outside of special education qualification.

Item number 2: Student who speaks multiple languages

Intervention: During the process of interviewing the family (and possibly the student), it is possible that the team will find information that indicates something that the student is struggling with that has a negative impact on their ability to focus on learning. This could be a cultural issue or trauma. If the student is a student who has suffered trauma, the team can find resources in the area for trauma treatment and provide the contact information to the family. If there is a cultural issue, the team can find a leader in the community of the family and ask for ideas and/or help to assist the student.

Red Flag Area! --- Item number 3: Native Language to Primary Language Transition

For this example, this is defined as: The student is unsure of which words go with which languages. For example, this might be a student that knows red is the correct word when they see something red, but does not know which language red goes with. This same student might know that something is azul when they see something blue, but they don't know which language azul goes with. This student might be able to pick out some of the colors if you ask the questions in Spanish, and other colors when you ask in English. The student might answer at times in English at times in Spanish. This is contrasted to randomly inserting English words into their Spanish or Spanish words into their English, which could be a lack of vocabulary in one language or the other, and for some students with stronger language skills this could be code switching.

Evaluation: During a special education evaluation, the team is taking their pre-referral data and combining the data with evaluation data. A student who is struggling with language development and transition across multiple languages in the home at 8 years of age is a supporting piece of data, yet not extremely strong. However, a 14-year-old student who has been exposed since birth to the two languages in question, and the exposure has been strong for both languages, whose siblings have none of the same problems, is a student for whom this piece of data is supportive of a potential disability if it converges with other similar data.

Red Flag Area! --- Item number 4: Education in Native/Primary language

Intervention: If the student has not had the exposure and experiences to formal education in their native language, they are missing the transferable skills from their language to the English language. They are also missing the school exposure in a language in which they always knew what was occurring. Therefore, if at all possible, we need to provide them support and learning opportunities in their native language. If there are things they can do in their native language, we need to find ways to make this work for them. Also, if we see them struggling with something that is a normal school activity, we need to assume they don't know what is expected instead of thinking they "can't" do it correctly. With this, we need to teach the skill and observe how quickly they learn the new skill. Part of the intervention can be the effective use of technology and translanguaging. Also, when designing a new lesson, think about the terms that are academic terms (vocabulary that is not as likely to occur in the home setting unless one of the parents is a teacher). Then, work with the ELL teacher to make sure that the students are exposed to this vocabulary and learn it prior to the new lesson.

Some of this is accomplished through screen readers that can translate the text into the native language of the student, and voice to text systems for numerous languages. Even Google Translate has improved to the point that it can be used successfully when some minimal caution is taken. Additionally, programs like CoWriter and Snap to Read can be very helpful.

Item number 5: Parental literacy in primary language

Intervention: Students for whom this is true need activities designed to build vocabulary. And, in most cases, would benefit from vocabulary building in both languages. If at all possible, use picture dictionaries that have both languages, then the vocabulary is more comprehensible and the parents can help with the vocabulary building (since they know the names of the items, even if they cannot read them). The final chapter provides further examples for intervening in this area.

Referral: If this was marked at or toward referral, it is because the student has literate parents and the student is struggling to learn academically. This is one point of data that helps the team understand that the student is having a struggle that does not appear reasonable given their exposure/experience/expectations/practice to vocabulary and language. Now, the team needs to compare and contrast this against the other points of data to see if the totality of information supports asking the parents to consent for a special education evaluation or not.

Item number 6: Student did not learn to read in the primary language

Intervention: More intervention is marked in this case because the student didn't have a reasonable opportunity to learn to read in their native language, and they are trying to learn to read in English while they are trying to learn English. Any type of native language support at this time would be very helpful. For example, being able to listen to the same story in their native language prior to needing to listen to or read it in English is going to increase comprehension. If they have the option of using an electronic device that can take portions of the text and translate them into their native language to listen to in their native language, that would be helpful. Some students just need help with a handful of words per page in their native language. Use technology so they can quickly find the meaning of that word in their native language (especially if they can hear the word). For the last two suggestions, iPhones and iPads have iTranslate available that can be used with voice (something very helpful for the teachers and front office staff when dealing with newcomers). Kindle books supports several languages in which a simple touch of the screen gives the reader the definition of the word in their native language.

Referral/Evaluation: This is about the student who had a strong experience regarding opportunity to learn to read in their native language and did not. This is made stronger when the parent tell you that siblings, or cousins, or classmates were all progressing strongly in reading and your student of concern was not.

Item number 7: Years learning English

Please note, we don't delay referrals to special education, even one day, for students who are language learners and have a disability that clearly has no relationship to language acquisition and almost always leads to special education services for native English speakers, like students who have blindness or deafness.

Evaluation: During a special education evaluation, the team takes their pre-referral data and combines it with evaluation data. If you have a student who has been in the school in the United States for 6-7 years and is doing poorly in school, you potentially have a student with a disability. In order to be able to use this to support a potential disability, you need to know more about the students in your school system who speak the same language as this student. If there is a group of LTELs (Long Term ELLs) who are not making progress in your system and not graduating at the same rate*, then this is not strong evidence toward supporting a disability (if the student of concern is part of this group). In contrast, students from very low incidence languages who are struggling have this data as supporting eligibility, given their need to learn English is much greater (investigate to make sure this is true for the student of concern).

*Systems level problem to address.

Item number 8: Attendance History

Intervention: If the student is not attending school, and you are able to determine that they are not attending due to school being a bad experience for them or because of a belief that school is not mandatory, then the team can work with the student to address their concerns. For example, if a student is not attending school because they have always done well in school and suddenly they are struggling, they need to be able to talk with others who have had the same experience and succeeded. These students need to know that studying in a new language and a new culture is a difficult task for everyone. If you have a student who is not attending due to a cultural belief that school is not important or is optional, then help them to see the options that can open up for them if they continue with school. Do not disparage their thinking, but instead provide them information on what is possible if they stay in school.

Referral: If you have a student who is struggling in school and school has always been difficult for this student, then the team needs to look for evidence that supports this claim. The stronger the evidence the more likely that a decision will be easier and clearer during the referral process. This is one point of data that helps the team understand that the student is having a struggle that does not appear reasonable given their exposure/experience/expectations/practice. Now, the team needs to compare and contrast this against the other points of data to see if the totality of information supports asking the parents to consent for a special education evaluation or not.

Red Flag Area! --- Item number 9: Your Data regarding Your ELL Services --- Results

It is not uncommon for students to struggle in a dual language program until early to late third grade (e.g., language confusion – this has many definitions and is being used here to address the natural process of a student learning enough in both languages to function in both languages) and then to perform at a much higher level (a delay versus a disability).

Referral: If you have a strong ELL system, **based upon data**, and you have a student who is doing poorly, then how strong is your data and how much does this support a potential disability and the need to complete a special education evaluation? The more the student is "sticking out" from other students, the more this supports moving forward, the less they "stick out," the more you would need strong indicators in other items to support moving forward. This is one point of data that helps the team understand whether or not the student's struggle appears reasonable given their exposure/experience/expectations/practice. Now, the team needs to compare and contrast this against the other points of data to see if the totality of information supports asking the parents to consent for a special education evaluation or not.

Evaluation: During a special education evaluation, the team takes their pre-referral data and combines it with evaluation data. The more the student is "sticking out" from other students, the more this supports moving forward, the less they "stick out", the more you would need strong indicators in other items to support the possibility of special education eligibility. For a student to "stick out" from other students in this context you would need data like: the percentage of language learners qualified for special education in the setting is much lower than the local/state averages and the school is very concerned regarding this student.

Red Flag Area! --- Item number 10: Rate of growth on the state language acquisition test

Evaluation: This is a key piece of data if you are evaluating a language learner who you believe might have a specific learning disability and has less than the 5-7 years learning English. This can be combined with other points of data as an indicator of how well this student learns in comparison to like peers. The farther below the rate of learning of their like peers, the stronger the data becomes. In contrast, the closer their rate of learning to their like peers, the weaker the data becomes. This requires strong peer likeness to improve the strength of the results.

Red Flag Area! --- Item number 11: Intervention Description

Intervention: This can be a key to either generating intervention ideas or to deciding in favor of a referral and possibly an evaluation. That is, if you complete a targeted intervention and the student performs in a manner similar to like peers your team needs to keep doing what they are doing.

In contrast....

Referral: This could be moderate to strong data for either the referral decision or during the evaluation process. If the student performed poorly on a targeted intervention when compared to like peers, and there is other supporting data to go from referral to proposing an evaluation for special education, then this could be a piece of data supporting that decision.

Targeted intervention is a key to understanding a student who you might believe there is a possibility of a specific learning disability, especially when the student is under that 5 years of experience learning English. However, if they are within an LTEL (Long-term ELL) group, the evaluations become much more difficult and the system needs to examine ways in which to reduce the quantity of LTEL students through more effective ELL services.

Red Flag Area! --- Item number 12: Expectations in the general education classroom

Intervention: The intervention in this case should be obvious, the team needs to work together to create reasonable expectations and a support system for the expectations (with reasonable modifications as the student's skills grow).

Item number 13: Classroom observation

Referral: If you have a student who is in a well-run classroom, who is trying to follow along with the other students, who is just not progressing in a manner similar to their like peers, your team needs to see whether or not there are other data points that indicate a similar trend. This is a potential piece of data that can be indicative of a student's rate of learning or ease of ability to learn. It would be important to note how other language learners are doing in the same classroom. The more unlike the other students this student is, the more supportive this data is of going from referral to proposing a special education evaluation. If there are other language learners in that setting who are struggling then this is not a strong piece of data.

Item number 14: Comparison Student Data

Evaluation: This is another key piece of data in the referral and evaluation process. This is especially important for the evaluations in which the team is looking at the possibility of a qualification in the category of specific learning disability for a student who has less than the 5-7 years of learning English. Again, the more unlike this student is than their true peers, the stronger this supports qualification. The less unlike this student is than their true peers, the less this supports qualification. A secondary example of this could be that the student has like peers (using the LE^{3}AP model) in 4 out of their 6 classes, and the student is the lowest performer of these language learner like peers in all 4 of the comparison groups.

The true peers or like peers need to be students who speak the same language and have been learning within our school system for the same amount of time. The more like the peers are on multiple variables, the stronger the comparison. The less like the peers are, the weaker the comparison. If you work in a small district, then work with neighboring small districts to create a spreadsheet that can be shared that allows for comparisons (non-identifiable). This can start with things like grade level, age, language, years in US school, and all available test scores. Then, add to this as needed or wanted. Also, students who speak rare languages are like peers to students who speak rare languages, given these students through data analysis have been shown less likely to be qualified for special education.

Item numbers 15 and 16:

For both of these items, the interventions are not likely to be designed from this new knowledge, but instead due to this new knowledge. In some cases (unless you find out about a medical condition previously unknown or the student clearly has a disability), you might go straight to intervention. For example, if you find out the student has never been in school before, it is likely that you need to find a way to get some of those early school experiences while getting age-appropriate experiences (in other words, to get more schooling). At other times, the data from these items could lead straight to evaluation. This could be finding out that the student has a medical condition that is almost always directly linked to a need for special education services.

During the writing of this 3rd edition, I inherited the case of a student with an intellectual disability who was relatively new to the United States. The evidence was very clear that moving forward with an evaluation was the correct decision. There will be times in which you are part of the way through the process and new evidence makes for an immediate need to go to interventions or an evaluation. That is a reasonable decision, if your evidence supports it.

Preschool Version

Please note, the first few items/examples are going to focus on interventions. For the later items the authors used more examples for "Referral" or "Evaluation." That is not because those items lead that direction to a greater degree, but instead to provide a balance of examples.

Exposure (1):

Intervention: In this case, if a child has not been exposed to a desired learning, or not exposed to the extent that other children who learned the skill have been exposed, then exposure is needed. There are times in which the lack of exposure is related to cultural issues. Therefore, the team needs to be respectful of this and think about alternative exposures that could provide the same skill development. For example, some mothers feed their children and do not encourage their children to feed themselves. This could lead to slower development of some fine-motor skills (and low scores on some of our rating scales and potentially have no relationship to a disability). Instead of debating with the parents regarding the choices they are making, the team could suggest toys that require fine-motor skills development. For items within the Preschool ELL CDP, using the activity noted within the final chapter can be an idea generator for both core instruction and interventions.

Experience (2):

Intervention: In this case, if a student has not had the experience, then they need the experience. The example above crossed over from Exposure to Experience by suggesting having the student play with different types of toys. This would not only give them the exposure, but also the experience (and do so in a fun way that they are likely to stay involved with, which adds in Practice).

Expectations in the household/daycare (3):

Intervention: In this case, there are times in which the parents need to be provided with ideas (interventions) so they understand the impact of their behaviors on reinforcing their children, for both the positive and not so positive results. For example, with children who grunt to get their needs met in place of using language, the parents are meeting the needs of the child without any expectations regarding attempting language, and the child really has little or no need to develop the skills. Therefore, the team (continued in item 4) can work with the parents regarding an intervention, and they would then create reasonable expectations for the child for the area of concern.

Intervention (Practice) Description (4):

Intervention: This example is continued from above. The team could help the parents to understand what key words to start expecting the child to produce (the highly motivating words related to the child getting their wants and needs met). The team could talk with the parents regarding reinforcing correct approximations, shaping the words with the child, and the fact that the child might have some tantrums when this is starting (given what they were doing was working for them and they cannot understand the need for a change).

Referral: The parent from the situation noted above, regarding speech, followed through with your recommendations and the child is still struggling. This would be a potential piece of data regarding marking referral in the matrix and processing the referral. If the discussions with the parent during the referral led to information that they were inconsistent, then the team might refuse to propose an evaluation (and work with the parents regarding the intervention). If the team learned that the parents were very consistent and the child made very little growth, the team might choose to propose an evaluation.

Evaluation: In this case, if there was a targeted intervention that was completed with fidelity and the child made much slower than expected growth (when compared to like peers), this could be a strong piece of data (depending upon the other sources of data and how well it either fits in with those pieces of data or does not).

Parental literacy in primary language (5):

Referral: If you find out that the parents have strong literacy skills, that they read with and talked with their child as they did with their other children, and their other children are developing as expected, yet this child is not, then you have strong evidence to combine with your other sources of data during the referral process. In other words, your major concern could be expressive and receptive language and you have one piece of evidence that is indicative of a language rich environment. Do you have other pieces of evidence to support this? Or, does the other evidence diverge?

Approach taken with regards to English Learning (6):

Evaluation: If you have a child who has had significant exposure to learning English, has motivation to learn English (loves the cartoons in English and wants to speak English with older siblings), but is struggling to learn English, then you might have evidence that supports the possibility that this child has a disability. The key issue is how this combines with other sources of data. If the other sources of data conflict with this, then the team needs to determine why (is there another cause for the problem that the team does/did not know).

Child's Primary Language, Environment, and Need to Learn English (7):

Referral: If you have a child who has a significant need to develop English language skills and has the exposure to these skills, and is not learning the English, then you have a piece of data that could support the referral process. For example, if the child speaks a native language that is extremely uncommon in your area (and nobody other than their family speaks this language) and the child is in a daycare environment in which nobody speaks their language, and they still are not learning English, this could be strong evidence during the referral process.

Observation (8):

Intervention: Your team completes an observation and the child behaves appropriately with children they have never seen before and listens to the requests of the adults (other than their parents) and completes the requests, then you probably need to discuss an intervention with the parents. That is, if a child can get along with children in general (just not their siblings) and listens well to adults (just not their parents), then someone needs to find the nicest way possible to point this out to the family. Then, if that goes well, the staff and parents can talk about parenting skills and strategies.

The Parent Interview (9 A) and Developmental History (9 B):

The parent interview and developmental history have the possibility of discovering information that leads directly toward intervention or evaluation. For example, if the team learns about a medical condition that almost always leads to the need for special education services, then the team might go directly to making a special education referral. In contrast, the team might learn about a history of trauma and work to find information and resources to link the family with.

Like in the K-12 process, each time the team looks at the skill that needs to be developed, they are trying to determine how to intervene upon developing that skill or how well this piece of data supports other pieces of data in the referral and/or evaluation process. Allow the student data, not your beliefs or preconceptions, to pick which path is travelled. Only your district student data will tell you how much your beliefs or your preconceptions have impacted your work ("you" meaning all people involved in the process). Overall, disproportionality is created by us, and therefore solved by us.

Appendix D: Biography and Training by Steve Gill

Steve Gill is available to provide 2 to 4-day training sessions on ELL and special education issues on a limited basis, but available for single day sessions on a regular basis. For more information, contact Steve through our website – stevegillell.com

Steve Gill Biography

Steve's first job in education, before he became a school psychologist, was as a driver's education teacher. Then Steve had the wonderful opportunity to study school psychology and work at the university, so he followed that path.

Steve started his career as a school psychologist in a district with a large ELL population. There he realized how little he had learned about language learners prior to this experience. Over the years, he completed graduate work in ELL studies, eventually creating the ELL Critical Data Process. As of writing this, Steve has trained over 21,000 educators on the process from more than 1,500 school districts in multiple states. The ELL Critical Data Process is being used in 12 countries that we know about at this time.

Steve and Ushani (Steve's wife and co-author) have six books, a booklet and a workbook for sale on Amazon.com.

- *The ELL Critical Data Process- Third Edition,* revised in 2023, is a resource used by educational professionals for determining whether more interventions are needed or if a special education referral is a reasonable option.
- *Evaluating ELL Students for the Possibility of Special Education Qualification* focuses on data analysis for language learners and how to potentially achieve appropriate identification rates. This book has been reduced in price, given updates in other books. The strength of this book is the data analysis and examples for reports.
- *Special Education Referral or Not*, is about using a matrix-based approach with non-language learners.
- *ELL Teachers and Special Education*, is a self-study or group study for ELL teachers to learn more about special education.
- *Processing Perspective, Examining Beliefs, Biases and Reality Through Stories*, is a book that uses educator stories to help people see different perspectives and analyze the lens we each look through to view the world.
- *Lessons Learned while Evaluating ELL Students for Potential Special Education Qualification*, is a book that provides practical steps and advice for those completing special education evaluations with language learners.

- There is also a workbook that goes with *The ELL Critical Data Process- Second Edition,* called *The Ell Special Education Evaluation Workbook (Companion and Training Document for the ELL Critical Data Process).*
- Our booklet, *Language Acquisition: Building a solid foundation and pursuing a new level of language mastery* is on language acquisition and provides the reader practical and concrete steps for building their students' or their own new language foundation. This is followed by practical steps to moving from foundational language to language mastery.

Steve is a Past President of the Washington State Association of School Psychologists.

Overview of the 2-Day Training Program (in person)

This is a commonly used option, based upon the "I Do, We Do, You Do" model of teaching.

Outline of Training

The training is designed using the "I Do, We Do, You Do" model. The first day focuses on participants learning the background information needed to move forward with the ELL Critical Data Process. The second day begins with covering the ELL Critical Data Process a second time, while stopping regularly to check for understanding and answer questions. The afternoon of the second day will have the participants applying their knowledge of the ELL Critical Data Process to two case studies in order to clarify any remaining questions and ensure correct understanding of the key concepts. Participants will complete the ELL Critical Data Process while defending their answers with the rubric and obtaining immediate feedback as the final check for understanding of the key concepts.

Day 1:

Section 1: The first section of the training covers background issues, problems, laws, and research needed to assist staff in addressing the belief systems of others, and their own belief systems, that are impacting the progress in this field. The content focuses on understanding the relationship between acculturation, belief systems, practices and results.

Section 2: The second section of the training addresses how children qualify for special education services with a focus on ELL specific issues that arise during qualification. This includes examples of how to reduce the problems and core issues that lead to disproportionality, while breaking down the problem to three main areas of qualification.

Section 3: The third section focuses on training those in attendance on how to complete the ELL Critical Data Process. This is the process created by Steve that helps staff to gather the most critical data, follow a structured process, and create a product that helps them to see whether more interventions are needed or if a special education referral is a reasonable option. The ELL Critical Data Process brings key staff members to the table and structures the discussions so that a student's needs are better understood.

Day 2:

Morning: The third section from above, focusing on the ELL Critical Data Process is repeated with the participants. There will be about 1 hour of additional time. To increase the understanding of the process and implementation of the process, the groups will be asked to have discussions frequently and asked to share their thoughts and questions to measure understanding.

Afternoon: The participants will work through 2 cases studies. The first one will be a real case from their schools and/or agency, using evaluation documents that have been redacted. This will be done in part to help increase the understanding of correct implementation of the ELL Critical Data Process and in part to help emphasize how critical it is to have, process, and document data within the process of determining whether or not a language learner has a disability. The second case study uses the ELL Critical Data Process Workbook to examine a real case completed by Steve. This case provides examples of wording to help the reader of the report understand if the student is struggling due to language acquisition issues or if the student has a disability and also happens to be a language learner.

A common 3-day training adds the Preschool ELL Critical Data Process Training

This option allows for a focus on preschool issues.

Section 1: The first section of the training covers background issues, problems, laws, and research needed to assist staff in addressing the belief systems of others, and their own belief systems, that are impacting the progress in this field. The content focuses on understanding the relationship between our acculturation, belief systems, practices and results.

Section 2: The second section focuses on training those in attendance on how to complete the Preschool Version of the ELL Critical Data Process. This is the process created by Steve that helps staff to gather the most critical data, follow a structured process, and create a product that helps them to see whether more interventions are needed or if a special education referral is a reasonable option. The Preschool Version of the ELL Critical Data Process brings key staff members to the table and structures the discussions so that a student's needs are better understood. The Preschool Version focuses less on measured data (given there is far less available) and more on specific comparisons of the child's development in key areas as compared to like peers' development in the same areas, focusing on the LE^{3}AP process. The LE^{3}AP process is a lens used to look at student struggles focusing on: Exposure, Experience, Expectations, and Practice. This is a theme in many of the books written by Steve and Ushani. It helps educators understand if the student's struggle is to be expected given these factors or if the student should not have the noted struggles given this lens.

2-day training requires 6 hours of contact time each day.

Preschool ELL CDP Training Day (approximately 4 ½-5 hours)

Online Training

Training Sections for Online training:

1. The ELL Critical Data Process K-12

This section focuses on training those in attendance on how to complete the ELL Critical Data Process. This is the process created by Steve that helps staff to gather the most critical data, follow a structured process, and create a product that helps them to see whether more interventions are needed or if a special education referral is a reasonable option. The ELL Critical Data Process brings key staff members to the table and structures the discussions so that a student's needs are better understood.

2. Preschool Version of the ELL Critical Data Process

This section focuses on training those in attendance on how to complete the Preschool Version of the ELL Critical Data Process. This is the process created by Steve that helps staff to gather the most critical data, follow a structured process, and create a product that helps them to see whether more interventions are needed or if a special education referral is a reasonable option. The Preschool Version of the ELL Critical Data Process brings key staff members to the table and structures the discussions so that a student's needs are better understood. The Preschool Version focuses less on measured data (given there is far less available) and more on specific comparisons of the child's development in key areas as compared to like peers' development in the same areas, focusing on the LE³AP process. The LE³AP process is a lens used to look at student struggles focusing on: Exposure, Experience, Expectations, and Practice. This is a theme in many of the books written by Steve and Ushani. It helps educators understand if the student's struggle is to be expected given these factors or if the student should not have the noted struggles given this lens.

3. The Evaluation Process for Language Learners (with an emphasis on integrating the ELL Critical Data Process Information)

This section of the training focuses on providing an overview of the techniques and steps outlined in our book *Lessons Learned While Evaluating ELL Students for Potential Special Education Qualification*. This is the culmination of 30 years of working on increasing the likelihood of finding students who truly have disabilities, versus the students whose struggles are primarily related to language acquisition. This section provides practical advice on how to help others, strangers to the situation, understand how the decision was made and what evidence was used. In the end, is the determinant factor language acquisition or language acquisition with a disability? This includes information needed to defend the decision within the special education eligibility report. This is legally required, as written in the

155

regulations, "**Ensure that information obtained from all of these sources is documented and carefully considered.**"

Feedback on Trainings, Process, and Books

Diversity and Social Justice Training Feedback

"I'd like to take this opportunity to thank you again for sharing your expertise with our members on March 21st at the Diversity and Social Justice Conference. As you can see from the feedback below, the participants were filled with insights and inspiration that will affect their practice. We appreciate your consideration to return as a speaker as we plan future offerings.   Thank you!!   C."

Feedback on Steve Gill's presentations – "Special Ed Qualification Issues with a Focus on ELL issues" and "The ELL Critical Data Process"

- All good! Great useful information and perspective from very knowledgeable, expert/professional – could be two-day training☺.
- Steve and Jeff were great, both content and delivery!
- Even though I do not teach a large number of ELL students, the things I learned can be directly applied to all students, regardless of background.
- I will use/take the information from the SPED/ELL breakout sessions in teaching, assessing, evaluating and potentially referring – or NOT – kids for SPED.

District Training Feedback:

"When you sit through one of Steve's Data Matrix trainings, it becomes extremely clear how much school districts have lacked the expertise and methods for carrying out referrals and evaluations on students who are English Language Learners. I personally learned more in the 2-hour session about English Language Learners than I ever did in graduate school or my own practice. His work is thorough, eye-opening, and most importantly, practical." AG, School Psychologist

"Hi, Steve. I can't thank you enough for such a great experience working with you. Beyond your knowledge, expertise, and the research base that you bring, you are so personal and engaging.

Additionally, your communication has always been amazing and your willingness to assist with 'extra questions/support'. For example, when I inquired about your understanding with IEPs from Puerto Rico and you recommended having a phone conversation. Your willingness to follow-up with items, essentially 'beyond the contract' is refreshing. You have been the easiest presenter I have worked with and had the best communication. You truly are about the kids and helping educators be better at our work. We've had excellent feedback on the learning, implementation, and your presentation style. Thank you, thank you!!" AM, Program Coordinator

"Steve uses research based content and district data in his presentation with both care and humor. He is conscientious to both recognize the passion of educators, while working to move them forward in their practice of evaluating students from second language backgrounds. This is such an important topic for staff and Steve's work is critical in helping to move our district forward in this area. The protocol that Steve has developed should be required of any team evaluating an ELL student for possible special education eligibility." KH, Asst. Director of Special Education

"Steve's presentation was clear, concise and built on foundational principles of Special Education, Civil Rights, and the science of language learning and was immediately relevant to the real work that we do every day as school practitioners facing complicated questions. His training and material was the catalyst that launched our district on a path toward more informed interventions for culturally and linguistically diverse students." BC, Special Services Coordinator

"I'm sorry it has taken me so long to thank you for your wonderful ELL Pre-referral Presentation for us here in Battle Ground. I have heard so many positive comments about your presentation and the protocol/matrix that you have created.

Everyone I spoke to, which included School Psychologists, Reading Specialists and ELL Specialists said they thought the protocol/matrix was the best they had ever seen and should be used for all students.

You presented such a wealth of information and made so many excellent comments! One thing I heard over and over was that everyone should have this training. They said they had gained valuable information that has changed how they view ELL students' language abilities and how they would assess ELL students in the future.

You are providing such a valuable service to the districts around the state and to our ELL students and families. We really are lucky to have your expertise.

Thank you for making the effort to come to our district and share your vast knowledge on the ELL Pre-referral process for ELL students."

JM, ELL Coordinator

"Your book is wonderful--a very much needed resource in an area of great need. Thanks for sending us a copy! Although we are not specialists in special education, we have done enough work with doctoral graduates who are bilingual special ed. experts to know that your book has a system for appropriate assessment that is very much more comprehensive than anything else we have seen to date. Wow, you have reached many educators in the state of Washington through this training and providing this book to them! And you can indeed be proud of your work, reducing the number of English learners assessed as needing special education services, across the state of Washington." VC, Professor, Researcher, Author

"Dear …,

I wanted to write to you to tell you how invaluable Steve Gill's training was for our District yesterday. He presented to 63 staff members who sit on our building Guidance Teams: Principals, Deans of Students, School Counselors, School Psychologists, and Speech/Language Pathologists. He presented for a full day on ELL and Special Education and then remained for extra time to offer examples and specific guidance for the process he has developed to our school psychologists. He was a compelling speaker, he easily engaged and held the attention of all of the participants. He cited research and used data throughout. He used our own District data to inform us about how we are addressing dually identified students (ELL/IDEA) in our District providing us a road map for improvement. I want to thank you for allowing Steve to bring this important knowledge and practice to other Districts.

Thanks so much, on behalf of our staff, and especially, our students."

SW, Special Education Director

"Thank you so very much for sharing such a wonderful presentation with Eastmont and our neighbors. Your insight is so valuable to our advocacy for diverse learners. I'm looking forward to teaming with our Special Education department to ensure students are appropriately served. You're responsible for bridging our services. What a huge benefit for our students!

Your wit, knowledge, and expertise made for such a worthwhile experience for all of us. Thank You!

We really appreciate your time and efforts."

AD, ELL Director

Made in the USA
Middletown, DE
15 August 2023

36784407R00088